Glenn Widelko is a learning facilitator and coach with a wealth of experience, working internationally across diverse brands and industries. His expertise centres on leadership development, performance management, relationship management and personal impact. Glenn's unique touch creates an exceptional learning environment that empowers individuals and groups to re-think their potential and inspires them to achieve their very best when it really matters. He is Director of WiDELKO Associates and divides his time between Cape Town, South Africa and the UK.

# THE
# STRETCH
# ZONE

## How to be confident when it really matters and achieve your performance potential

*'I probably haven't truly believed in myself until now.'*
**Siofra O'Smotherly, Award Winning Manager**

*'The most positive and amazing thing I have ever learnt.'*
**Bev Grimshaw, Coaching Client**

## Glenn Widelko

Balloonview

Printed in the United Kingdom for Balloon View Ltd by
CPI Group (UK) Ltd, Crodon, CR0 4YY

ISBN 978-1-907798-20-7

*To my parents*
*Erica & Kazimierz*

*To my friend and wife, Sheelagh*
*and sons Matthew & Andrew*

# References

'The stretch zone has helped me see my confidence and potential quite differently. It has put me in a very different space where I'm no longer holding myself back and avoiding difficult situations.'

### Alan Lamond, Senior Manager – Financial Services

'Glenn's coaching around removing self-doubt has had a huge effect on my performance and interactions with others. Rediscovering my inner confidence has seen me take on new situations and difficult conversations in a way I never thought I could. The insights within this very different approach have made such a difference.'

### Geoff Mason, Director Business Banking – Financial Services

'I guess I just want to thank you. I've experienced some positive changes since our last session - a quiet confidence I guess. The doubt obviously still creeps in from time to time, but I can recognise it now for what it is. I also just feel so much more relaxed, almost too relaxed!!'

### Cindy Malga, IT Consultant

'Once I'd heard that confidence is the absence of doubt it just made sense. It was as if a light went on. And I now have the proof that I am as capable as anyone and can manage some really strong personalities. I wish I had done this ten years ago.'

### Liz Giles, Regional Director – Financial Services

'The leadership programme with Glenn has been 'life changing'. Seeing my confidence differently has enabled me to manage difficult situations with renewed perspective. I am now clear on what confidence really is (and isn't) and the good news is that I now have some simple things to do to feel more confident more often.'

### Paul Hulcoop, Business Risk Manager – Financial Services

'Glenn is a master-facilitator with the knack of locating the real issues that hinder learners from reaching their potential, enabling people to transcend their limitations in his quietly challenging way. His ability to coach and facilitate are at a level I have rarely seen in three decades.'

**Vanessa Witten, Managing Partner – Just in Time Learning Solutions**

'As a leadership facilitator and coach Glenn has a remarkable capacity to deeply connect with people straight away. Based on this connection is his ability to ask tough questions and share observations that have really made me stop and think. The outcome is real insight, personally and professionally.'

**Richard Wilson, Director – Financial Services**

'For me, Glenn is very much a Zen facilitator. The way he expresses himself in his calm quietness creates a powerful environment for learning, as people stop and listen. His warm touch and focused approach place the learner at the centre of a very dynamic experience.'

**Etienne Joudon, Manager – Financial Services**

'Confidence really is the absence of doubt. What I have found is a renewed level of impact as people are really listening to and hearing me. It is as if a weight has lifted and I've given myself permission to be myself.'

**Paul Fletcher, Director – Financial Services**

'Glenn is a tremendous coach and he does it in such an unassuming way. He listens with such depth and when he does say something it is always so incisive.'

**Grahame Major, Relationship Director – Financial Services**

'Glenn exudes the confidence that he talks, coaches and teaches about, in a way that is authentic, honest and rare in the age of bigger and bolder.'

**Karen White, Professional Coach**

'Glenn's confidence coaching has given me a real 'eureka' moment – for the first time I feel I have real clarity on what confidence actually is, and how I can use and apply this knowledge to overcome challenges and make me an even better leader.'

**Steve Southworth, Director Business Banking – Financial Services**

'Something really clicked for me in the coaching with Glenn. I'd spent years searching for real confidence without realising it was inside me all along. Seeing confidence quite differently I now know exactly how to simply be confident.'

**Becky Driscoll, Business Risk Manager – Financial Services**

'The stretch zone has given me the tools to change my life – it just hadn't occurred to me that confidence is actually within us all and it is our self-doubt that holds us back.'

**Liz McEwan, Portfolio Risk Manager – Financial Services**

'As a facilitator Glenn leads you to push yourself to places you didn't know existed within you. I have never known any other personal development experience that leaves you feeling so challenged – a hugely beneficial investment, both personally and professionally.'

**John McParland, Director of Business Banking – Financial Services**

'The confidence coaching with Glenn has made such a difference. While I've always felt my confidence existed within me, my inner demons of doubt have held me back. I now have the tools to channel my efforts and energy differently and everything has fallen into place.'

**Danny Plows, Director of Assess Finance – Financial Services**

# Acknowledgements

Thank you to the many wonderful people that I've had the opportunity to work with as a coach and learning facilitator over the past 15 years. I have learnt so much from you and, without you, The Stretch Zone would not have been possible.

Thank you to the wonderful community of consultants, facilitators and coaches I've had the privilege of working with over the years in South Africa and the United Kingdom. I have thoroughly enjoyed your good company.

Thank you to Siofra O'Smotherly, Bev Grimshaw, Helen Cambell-Watt, Janice Byrne, James Hodkinson, Andy Brown, Marilouise Hughes, Martin Dickie, Andrew Taylor, Paul Jones, Richard Blyth, Karen Bradley, Demi Agrotis, Veronica Marnell, Tanya Gallagher, Karen Russell, Richard Sawyer, Jenny Hyatt, Alison Taylor, Jennifer Girven, Thomas Walker and Duncan Schofield.

Thank you to Sheelagh Widelko, Nigel Gilkes, Gillian Frame, Keith Dixon, James Hodkinson, Helen Cambell-Watt, Steve Harvey, Derek Eaton, Karen Grant, Vanessa Witten, Wanda Coustas, Glen Adams and Ernest Harvey for taking the time to read sample chapters and provide me with encouraging and constructive feedback.

Thank you to Nick Williams for your guidance and experience, to Sue Lascelles for editing The Stretch Zone and to Ed Peppitt for publishing The Stretch Zone. I have learnt and benefitted so much from each of you.

And thank you to my mentors and tutors for helping me to begin to discover within myself that timeless teaching, a wealth which is beyond measure.

# Contents

# Introduction

Make no mistake: you are already confident in full measure! Without exception we are, each and every one of us, imminently confident right here and right now. Our innermost confidence is limitless, authentic, real and sustainable. It is our constant companion, accessible anywhere, anytime, whose potential exceeds even our wildest aspirations. Yet, our capacity to be confident is all too often compromised by a fundamental mistake.

In our modern world we have gotten ourselves into such a hurry, burdening ourselves with pressures and predicaments in all manner of diverse contexts. And under the strain of these relentless pressures, our confidence so often seems to disappear when we need it most. Mistaking our fears and doubts about confidence for who we really are, we come to believe with increasingly entrenched conviction that confidence is something we lack. Believing we lack confidence, we hold ourselves back, distrust ourselves and never realise the innate talents and capabilities that lie brimming at the threshold of our innermost potential.

In truth, confidence is not something we lack or need to learn and acquire. Confidence is our natural state: an inherent potential for everyone without exception. When we no longer mistake ingrained convictions about ourselves for who and what we really are, we discover a very different potentiality, an openness and opportunity within ourselves – and we need never look back.

### Confidence – A New Paradigm

This book is based on my experience as a coach and learning facilitator, working with seasoned leaders across diverse brands and industries over the past fifteen years. As a coach and facilitator, I was initially intrigued by how often confidence emerged as an area for development. What was particularly interesting was that this was as true of people who seemed to exude confidence as it was of those who clearly lacked it. The bottom line is that confidence is an issue for everyone who has the courage to step outside their comfort zone.

So I found myself asking lots of questions. What is confidence? How does it work? Where does it come from? How can we be so confident in some situations and yet lack confidence in others? What makes confidence appear and disappear? Where does it appear from and where does it disappear to? Why do we appear to have so little control over our levels of confidence? How can we be confident in full measure, anywhere, anytime?

With questions, answers started to come – with certain patterns of behaviour, misconceptions and insights becoming increasingly apparent. I began to test out these observations in my coaching and the response over the years has been staggeringly positive. Comments such as 'this has really changed my life' have become commonplace; and yet within easy reach of all of us mere mortals.

What made the difference was the discovery of the insights and principles upon which this book is based. These insights and principles fundamentally challenge our assumptions about the underlying nature of confidence, creating a completely different paradigm of possibility. When combined with the practices as presented in this book, understanding this paradigm has helped the people I've coached to see through their preconceptions and discover a reservoir of confidence from within, enabling them to stand out from the crowd, take opportunities fearlessly and achieve what they previously thought was beyond their performance potential.

If you find yourself outside your comfort zone, in the face of adversity, this book will provide you with a unique understanding that will enable you to truly trust yourself, remember yourself, accept yourself and to be yourself and enjoy yourself when and where it really matters – rather than hold yourself back through self-limiting beliefs. The best person you can be is yourself, and when you truly trust yourself a very different paradigm of possibility becomes a tangible reality for you.

**So if you find:**

1. Your confidence holds you back, so you achieve less than your potential ...

2. Your confidence feels like hard work, draining your energy and impact ...

3. Your confidence comes and goes, disappearing when you need it most ...

...this book will provide you with the insights and techniques that, with diligent practice, will enable you to transform your life, your aspirations and potential.

The Stretch Zone will take you on a journey that more or less follows the professional coaching experience upon which it is based. In this way, the chapters unfold in much the same way that the coaching experience would unfold. While many, the chapters are short and sweet, written with the intention that they are quick and easy to read and you can absorb the principles and practices in bite-sized chunks.

As an experiential guide, each chapter begins with a question that aims to get you thinking about your own understanding and experience. You might like to keep a journal, tracking your understanding as it evolves in tandem with your progress through the book. Each chapter ends with an *In Summary* box which provides an easy-to-use reference point. You will find hundreds of helpful insights offered within these boxes in *The Stretch Zone*.

Throughout the book you'll also find real-life quotes from coaching clients, reflecting their understanding and responses to the insights, principles and practices presented within *The Stretch Zone*. While *The Stretch Zone* emerged from work I've done within a leadership development capacity, the insights, principles and practices are entirely relevant and applicable to any walk of life. The insights you will discover within this book are universal and will work within any context: at home, at work, on the sports field, on stage, in everyday situations and relationships – whenever you may find yourself outside your comfort zone and tested within the Stretch Zone.

Everything that I've heard coaching clients say over the years about their challenges with confidence I can recognise from my own experience. As a quietly spoken and reflective individual, I have never been one of those super-confident people who ooze confidence left, right and centre. Confidence is something that I've needed to discover for myself – and yet in my chosen profession it is absolutely essential. So this book reflects a very personal journey of self-discovery that I have enjoyed sharing with my clients. Like so many of my clients, I have found an inner calm and composure that enables me to be at my best even when I am well and truly out of my comfort zone.

The fact that this book draws not only from my professional experience, but also from a very personal journey, has afforded me a unique position from which to write about *being confident* in the Stretch Zone. Whenever we write, speak or teach about things that have never been an issue for us, we often lack the personal touch, insight and authenticity that can only come from direct experience, and the humility and empathy that accompany this. Every insight, principle and practice that is contained within this book is something that I've come to know and practise myself through direct experience. These discoveries have since become constant friends and companions that are always there for me whenever I need them most.

**Sizzle and Substance**

You need to be aware that this book comes with a health warning: it is not intended to be comfortable! The intention is to challenge you, to make you stop and think, and question the ideas, experiences and assumptions that you may seldom pause to question. Rather than going down the well trodden path of confidence-boosting hype, this book aims to challenge your assumptions and turn your understanding of confidence completely on its head.

*The Stretch Zone* makes a distinction between sizzle and substance. The sizzle is the showy stuff on the outside that is intended to dazzle. The substance is the essence within, the bedrock underlying everything else. When we attempt to develop confidence through clever little tricks that look good on the outside, the effect is not much more than a peripheral impact which soon fades due to the lack of substance behind the facade.

In contrast, when we focus on the substance, the confidence that results is real and sustainable – and is not likely to disappear when we need it most. Following this, *The Stretch Zone* demonstrates the underlying nature of confidence and enables everyday people to discover a reservoir of confidence within themselves, which can be accessed anywhere, anytime.

**Uniquely Different**

So what makes *The Stretch Zone* uniquely different from all the other books available on the enigmatic subject of confidence? Well, what makes this book profoundly different in my view is that it cuts to the chase and goes directly to the heart of the matter. As opposed to the sort of empty hype that purports to boost, build and develop confidence or enable people to *have* confidence – thereby prompting the flawed strategy of *having confidence* – *The Stretch Zone* is about discovering what is already there in abundance and releasing that which is your birthright from within you. *The Stretch Zone* is about *being confident*.

Confidence is not something that we can *have*. Confidence is only something we can *be*. Confidence is a state, a state of being. We cannot have confidence for tomorrow's difficult situation; we can only be confident in a place and time called here and now.

Nobody can make you confident. Confidence is not something that any of us can have and give to someone else as though it were an object. At best, others might be able to boost our confidence in some way. Yet, experience has taught me that confidence is seldom authentic, convincing or sustainable if dependent on someone or something else. *The Stretch Zone* is uniquely different as it enables everyday people to release a genuine confidence from within themselves. And, coming from within, that confidence is available to us anywhere and anytime.

What *The Stretch Zone* does not do is:

1. Give people a feeling of confidence. Confidence is already within us, a largely untapped potential.

2. Psyche people up with confidence-boosting hype, which is inauthentic and neither convincing nor sustainable.

3. Provide 101 clever tips and tricks to 'fake it till you make it', which seldom works.

What *The Stretch Zone* does do is:

1. Challenge your assumptions about confidence and your performance potential.

2. Provide the insights and practices that enable authentic confidence in the Stretch Zone.

3. Provide an integrated model which, once understood, can be summed up in just a few words.

Confidence and a healthy sense of self-esteem are not limited to only certain types of individual by virtue of their personalities. Without exception, confidence is an inherent potential for all of us, regardless of our personality or experience; it only looks and sounds different. *The Stretch Zone* enables people to create the conditions within which confidence is inevitable anywhere, anytime.

> 'Without exception, confidence is an inherent potential for all of us, regardless of our personality or experience; it only looks and sounds different.'

If issues about confidence are not affecting you in some way, the chances are you are spending too much time in your comfort zone. In my experience, even people who would typically be described as confident quickly disclose in a coaching context that confidence is an issue for them, with their fear being that people will see through them and 'see me for who and what I really am'.

We all have a Stretch Zone and while this may be different for different people and change for each of us over time, our capacity to be at our best is directly dependent on our ability to master our confidence in that Stretch Zone. As we step up with authentic confidence we will find renewed energy, presence, composure, focus and a resilient sense of self-esteem which enables our talents, relationships and aspirations to reach a new level and impact.

## One Last Thing

The one ingredient I cannot put into this book, but which is possibly the most important factor, is practice. To enable lasting change, you will need to put the principles and techniques in these pages into practice and come to your own understanding of what works and what does not work for you. With direct experience, true learning and capability will follow, with a real and sustainable change in your confidence, impact and potential.

If you can relate to what has been described above, *The Stretch Zone* has the potential to transform your life, enabling you to achieve your aspirations at work and play.

---

**In Summary**

1. Confidence is an issue for so many because of a fundamental mistake we make.

2. People who seem to exude confidence also seek help to develop their confidence.

3. We so seldom pause to question our assumptions about confidence and our potential.

4. Confidence is a state – a state of being – not something we can *have*, or possess, or hold on to.

5. Confidence is an imminent potential for all of us, regardless of our personality or experience.

---

Part One
# Our Day-to-Day Experience

## 1. Confidence – the Differentiating Factor

When was the last time you had an opportunity to make an impact, yet you held back your initial spontaneity with caution and hesitation? Instead you did nothing at all, or perhaps you did something but hesitantly. What effect did that have? How did it feel? What did it tell you about yourself? While your initial impulse to action was clear and certain, what followed was characterised instead by caution and hesitation.

On the other hand, when was the last time you seized an opportunity with unexpected spontaneity and, without caution or hesitation, you dealt with things as they developed? What was that like? How did that feel? What impact did that have? What did it say about you? Isn't it strange that in some situations we feel limitless and certain, while in others we feel hesitant and cautious?

> **Key Question:**
>
> In what situations do you tend to feel limitless and certain, and in what situations do you tend to feel hesitant and uncertain?

We are all, without exception, capable and confident beyond measure. Yet, when it really matters, we do not always feel that way. As opportunities arise, our natural spontaneity and performance potential seem to go out of the window and we hold ourselves back, undermining our capability and impact. Opportunities don't stick around and so we find ourselves missing them with self-recrimination and regret.

Unlocking our potential begins, first and foremost, with ourselves. The bottom line is that, when it really matters, what holds us back most is no one other than ourselves. We are so often our own worst enemies, inadvertently limiting our performance potential. Our readiness to step up and seize opportunities defines our impact and potential.

> 'Unlocking our potential begins, first and foremost, with ourselves.'

Confidence is the differentiating factor. Whether you are a senior leader, middle or junior manager, fresh talent on the way to great things, a salesperson, account manager, technical expert or professional helper, a sportsperson, musician or actor, when it matters most your inner state of confidence has a *direct and immediate* impact on your aspirations and potential. The impact your confidence has on your performance potential is not optional, it is a given. And it either enables or inhibits you.

> 'When it matters most, your inner state of confidence has a direct and immediate impact on your aspirations and potential.'

### Performance Stretch Curve

Anyone can be confident in their comfort zone. When we are in our comfort zones it doesn't really matter as we're never really tested anyway. Our comfort zones and our full potential are mutually exclusive. No one ever performs at their best when in the snooze zone. Performing at the edge of our capabilities demands instead that we step out of our comfort zones – into the Stretch Zone. The Stretch Zone demands that we be at our very best, and tests our talents and capabilities.

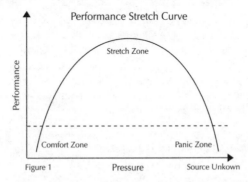

Figure 1

When it really matters, we will find ourselves standing at the threshold of the Stretch Zone, in unfamiliar territory. And yet, under the increased pressure of the Stretch Zone our confidence so often seems to desert us, disappearing into the ether, and we hold ourselves back, delivering less than our performance potential. What causes this is the underlying fear that we'll end up in the panic zone – the point at which we no longer feel we are able to cope.

The 'Performance Stretch Curve' demonstrates that, as we step up into the Stretch Zone, a degree of increased pressure has the effect of bringing out the best in our performance potential (see Figure 1). This element of pressure raises us out of our comfort zone and gives us an opportunity to shine; the pressure has to be quite considerable before we find ourselves plummeting down into the panic zone. However, in our fear and doubt we just do not trust ourselves and hold ourselves back unnecessarily at the outset of the process. Most of the performance pressure comes from within ourselves. Mastering the Stretch Zone is about mastering our confidence within that area of high performance. Confidence really is the differentiating factor.

Without exception, we all have a Stretch Zone, a place within which we feel vulnerable, exposed and where there is a substantial pressure on us to be at our best. To be at our best and achieve our aspirations, we have no choice but to step out of our comfort zone into unfamiliar and uncomfortable territory, and that means stepping into the Stretch Zone. Confidence within the Stretch Zone is what differentiates us from the crowd and facilitates our very best when it really matters.

**In Summary**

1. Confidence has a *direct and immediate* impact on our performance potential.

2. No one performs at their best in their comfort zone.

3. Confidence is the differentiating factor that enables us to perform to our best in the Stretch Zone.

4. Without exception, we all have a Stretch Zone and confidence is always the differentiating factor that determines our performance within it.

## 2. *Inside Out* vs. *Outside In*

*The Stretch Zone* presents a proven approach to rediscovering and releasing the reservoir of confidence that we all have without exception. Releasing confidence can be approached in one of two ways: by working from the *inside out* or from the *outside in*.

---

**Key Question:**

How would you differentiate between an *inside out* and an *outside in* approach to developing confidence?

---

An *inside out* approach means that, in order to make a sustainable impact on our *outer* performance, we need to begin with our *inner* performance. Our outer performance is directly dependent on our inner performance and always will be. So what do we mean by our inner performance?

---

'Our outer performance is directly dependent on our inner performance and always will be.'

---

Our inner performance refers to the combined effect that our thoughts, feelings, ideas, assumptions, attention, perception, identity, attachments, esteem and awareness have on our confidence and performance potential. An inside out approach cuts to the chase and takes us right to the heart of the matter, beginning with where the issue of confidence starts in the first place, and that is with our inner performance.

You may at first be inclined to challenge this idea. For example, many might argue that their lack of confidence has its roots in childhood in, say, a relationship with a hyper-critical father or mother. When I was coaching Paul, a senior manager, he commented that: 'I had a strict upbringing as a child and this had an impact on my confidence.' In this instance, we might assume that Paul's low confidence began with his relationship with his parents and, on a certain level, that makes some sense. However, in my experience, if Paul were to try to release his confidence by focusing exclusively on the past and his early relationship with his parents, this would have a highly limited and unsustainable effect.

While Paul's low confidence might have initially begun with his past relationship with his parents, his lack of confidence in the present actually begins anew each day within himself, as he plays and re-plays that dysfunctional relationship and lack of confidence in his mind over and over again. We each create and re-create the conditions whereby we habitually undermine our confidence and performance potential. So when we say that an inside out approach begins at the source, we are not talking about the past, but about our conditioned behaviours in the present.

> 'We each create and re-create the inner conditions whereby we habitually undermine our confidence and performance potential.'

An *outside in* approach, on the other hand, means focusing on observable behaviours such as body language, vocals, gestures, posture and the like. It also involves external initiatives such as setting goals, enjoying rewards, asking for feedback, wearing new business clothes, reading famous quotes, making resolutions, doing relaxation exercises, going for a run, convincing ourselves of our capabilities, psyching ourselves up, and so on.

However, when we develop confidence from the *outside in*, the change is only peripheral, a facade that is just not sustainable. It is like building a house on sand: the foundations are unlikely to sustain the building. But when we build confidence from the *inside out* we are actually developing the substance and foundations that will support our feelings of confidence anywhere and anytime.

This is not to throw the baby out with the bathwater and dismiss an *outside in* approach completely. The *outside in* approach most certainly has its place. Yet, when used in isolation, it seldom brings about real and sustainable change. In contrast, when used in support of an *inside out* approach, the combined effect is considerable. The real substance and best results, however, are reached through beginning with an *inside out* approach upon which everything else is dependent.

**In Summary**

1. Our *outer performance* is directly dependent on our *inner performance*.

2. We create and re-create the conditions whereby we undermine our confidence.

3. Real and sustainable confidence begins with an *inside out* approach.

4. *Outside in* initiatives bear fruit when used in support of an *inside out* approach.

## 3. Confidence: Our Day-to-Day Experience

Whenever confidence comes up in a coaching conversation, I typically ask: 'To what extent do you see yourself as a confident person?' What I have found is that people will respond in a remarkably similar way, with a very distinct pattern having emerged in my work over the past fifteen years.

**Key Question:**

To what extent do you see yourself as a confident person?

The response to this question, while expressed differently, is almost always very similar in substance. What people generally say is that they see themselves as confident and yet – within the very same breath – they will then partially negate what they have just said and say more or less the opposite: that they are not very confident. There are, of course, those who start by saying that they are not very confident and then negate this by coming round to the view that they are indeed confident. Either way, this is such a typical response and reflects a distinct pattern in our day-to-day experience of confidence.

In the course of my coaching work, three distinct observations have become apparent to me:

1. Without exception, we have all experienced moments of both high and low confidence.

2. Our experiences of high or low confidence are circumstantially dependent.

3. The circumstances that enable or disable confidence are different for different people.

The good news is that, because confidence manifests itself in certain situations for most of us, this implies that it must already be present somewhere within our system – or else it could not have manifested itself in the first place. However, we need to understand what it is that makes our own confidence show up in some circumstances but not in others. Once we understand this, we will be in a strong position to self-regulate our confidence in *The Stretch Zone*, when and where it matters most.

**In Summary**

1. Our day-to-day experience of confidence follows a distinct pattern.

2. Without exception, we have all experienced moments of high and low confidence.

3. Our experiences of high or low confidence are circumstantially dependent.

4. The circumstances that enable or disable confidence are different for different people.

## 4. Circumstantial Confidence

When asked, people are often unclear as to whether they see themselves as confident or not. Very seldom have I come across someone who has given a direct 'yes' or 'no' answer to this question. I can certainly identify with this from my own personal experience, and, had I been asked the same question before I began this work, I'm quite sure that I would have responded in much the same way.

Our general experience is that of *circumstantial confidence*, where our confidence comes and goes depending on the circumstances. While this is not rocket science, it is a very simple yet relentless pattern.

> 'Our general experience is that of circumstantial confidence, where our confidence comes and goes depending on the circumstances.'

> **Key Question:**
>
> What examples of circumstantial confidence can you think of from your own experience?

The question is: upon what or which circumstances is our confidence dependent? When we can answer this, we stand a good chance of being able to do something about it. The exact circumstances that release or undermine confidence will naturally be different for different people, depending on their character, preferences and life experience (see Figure 2). Before we explore this we need to recognise that circumstantial confidence can be viewed from two different perspectives, relating to our inner and outer worlds.

### Circumstantial Confidence – Two Perspectives

Confidence is, on the one hand, dependent on our outer *circumstances*. Our outer circumstances refer to whatever is happening within our environment. We might, for example, be

## Circumstantial Confidence

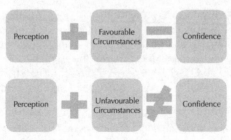

Figure 2

making a presentation in front of a large group, or having to stand up for ourselves in a shopping mall, or lining up to run the 100 metres. In some outer circumstances we feel fearless and certain, and yet in others we feel hesitant and uncertain.

However, confidence is also dependent on our *inner circumstances*. Our inner circumstances refer to our inner state of mind, heart, our perceptions, self-identity, awareness and the like. We might, for example, wake up one morning feeling really foggy and find that we just can't focus that day. We might subsequently feel frustrated or down, and not very confident at all. We might have had a near-accident while driving and sometime later still feel quite shaken up and less sure of ourselves. While the outer incident, the accident, has passed, our confidence is still affected by our mental and emotional states. It's clear that our level of confidence is very much influenced by both our inner and outer circumstances.

Further observation demonstrates that our inner and outer circumstances are interdependent. What we think and feel can be influenced by our outer circumstances. In the same way, our outer circumstances can reflect our inner state. We perceive external events through the filters of our thoughts, feelings, beliefs, paradigms and value judgements, for example, and these filters in turn influence what we see and how we behave.

The same situation can be viewed differently depending on our given state at the time. If we are in a sunny mood, for example, we tend to see things positively. When in a serious mood, we see our environment in a more sombre way. The key is our internal perception and the extent to which we project our inner state onto our circumstances. While the circumstances do not necessarily change in the real world, our perception and experience of them in our own private world can change dramatically – and so often does.

> 'The key is our internal perception and the extent to which we project our inner state onto our circumstances.'

---

**Example: a Presentation**

If we were presenting at a meeting and we were to observe someone walk out midway, this might throw us off-course – depending on our perception of the situation. If we think the person is leaving because of the quality of our presentation, our confidence is likely to be much more rattled than if we were to take the view that the person is leaving to go to the bathroom. These subtle processes of projection and perception are what make our outer circumstances a reflection of our inner state.

---

So what does all this mean in practice? Does it have any practical value at all, or is this just a matter of intellectual gymnastics? Experience has taught me that understanding the circumstantial nature of our day-to-day experience of confidence is an important step when it comes to releasing our authentic confidence from within.

### Implications in Practice

While my own experience and that of my coaching clients suggests that our day-to-day experience is one of circumstantial confidence, it is important for you to observe this for yourself. With a little reflection, it usually becomes immediately apparent; indeed, in the exercises in Chapter 1 and at the start of this chapter you will have explored this already. First, you identified those situations in which you feel hesitant and cautious and those situations in which you feel *limitless* and certain. Then you looked at situations that you know to involve circumstantial confidence.

It is important to recognise that while most of us are able to recognise the circumstantial nature of our confidence in retrospect, we are usually not so aware of it and the effect it has at the time – the *moment of impact*. And yet that effect is substantial and relentless.

When I was coaching Janice, a senior leader at a well known corporation, she reflected that her feeling of confidence was 'not stable but goes up and down'. Another client, Andy, put it very directly when he said, 'I am situation confident, rather than personally confident.' Our confidence seems to come and go depending on the situation. Further coaching with Janice demonstrated that her varying levels of circumstantial confidence had the effect of exacerbating her overall feelings of low confidence. The reason for Janice was that she could never be certain if confidence would be there for her in her *Stretch Zone* when she needed it most. As for the majority of us, the result of this kind of doubt is a spiral of low confidence, with uncertainty breeding further uncertainty.

> 'The effect is a negative spiral of low confidence with uncertainty breading further uncertainty.'

What exacerbates this even further is that, when in the Stretch Zone, we do not feel in control of our confidence. It is like being in the front seat of a car with a dummy steering wheel. No matter how hard we try to steer, our efforts seem to have no effect at all. The way in which our confidence comes and goes seems to be a matter of circumstance and not our free choice. In effect, we are left at the mercy of our circumstances. This is a situation that is neither very satisfactory nor conducive to developing real and sustainable confidence.

### A Sense of Dissatisfaction

While we might have learnt to cope with circumstantial confidence in our different ways, for many of us there remains an underlying sense that something is not quite right, that something

is missing. We are never really satisfied and we have a conscious or unconscious yearning for something better that seems within our grasp, yet just out of reach. And so the pattern continues.

It is interesting to note that confidence typically only becomes an issue when it is not there. It is as if we know it by its absence. When we feel confident we never question it, as if confidence were a state that is both normal and expected. Only when it is lacking do we feel that something is not quite right.

**In Summary**

1. The term *circumstantial confidence* implies our confidence comes and goes circumstantially.

2. Circumstantial confidence depends on both our inner and outer circumstances.

3. Confidence often *seems* to be a matter of circumstance and not personal choice.

4. Circumstantial confidence exacerbates our feelings of low confidence.

## 5. A Knee-Jerk Reaction

If we rely solely on circumstantial confidence, we can never be certain if our confidence will be there when we need it most. And with circumstantial confidence it so often isn't. To make matters worse, if our confidence depends more on our circumstances than our free choice, our feelings of doubt and inadequacy will be exacerbated substantially.

---

**Key Question:**

How do you react when your confidence seems to desert you in the Stretch Zone?

---

If our confidence disappears into the ether when we are faced with adversity, we will frequently react emotionally with fear and inadequacy. The speed with which these emotions arise is incredible and far quicker than our ability to think rationally. Inevitably accompanying fear in the heart is a whole lot of doubt in the mind, and the scene is set for *fight*, *flight* or *freeze*.

When in the Stretch Zone, some people will put on a bold front through a show of aggression: a *fight* reaction. Others may *freeze* and do nothing at all, like a rabbit caught in the headlights. And there will be those who adopt a *flight* reaction, avoiding the situation as far as possible. Many of us may end up doing a bit of all three, depending on our predicament and the options available to us.

All three reactions reflect low confidence and are nothing other than conditioned habits that we have learnt and internalised in our formative years and adult experience. Because these reactions have 'helped' us cope in the past, the coping mechanisms they offer will have become internalised as a part of who we think we are, our ego-identity (see Chapter 33). What follows is an entrenched idea that, for example, 'I am not a confident person' – an idea to which we become highly emotionally attached.

The coping mechanisms of fight, flight or freeze are, however, only a reaction to a preceding reaction. They are not the source and cause of our lack of confidence. The underlying knee-jerk reaction is the fear and doubt that arises within the heart and mind respectively, and this is what upsets the apple cart, undermining our confidence and composure.

**Mental and Emotional Hijacking**

When confronted with adversity we become mentally and emotionally hijacked through a knee-jerk reaction of fear and doubt, which incapacitates our faculties. Our ability to think clearly, speak freely, feel composed and behave appropriately becomes significantly undermined (see Figure 4).

> 'When confronted with adversity we become mentally and emotionally hijacked, through a knee-jerk reaction of fear and doubt, which incapacitates our faculties.'

While much has been said about emotional hijacking, very little has been said about its twin, mental hijacking. In the Stretch Zone we may find ourselves thinking incessantly: *What do I need to do? What might happen? What happened last time? Who is watching? Will I make a fool of myself? Do I have enough information? What are other people thinking? What will they think of me? Am I good enough? Will they listen to me? Will I achieve what I want to achieve?*

Mental & Emotional Hijacking

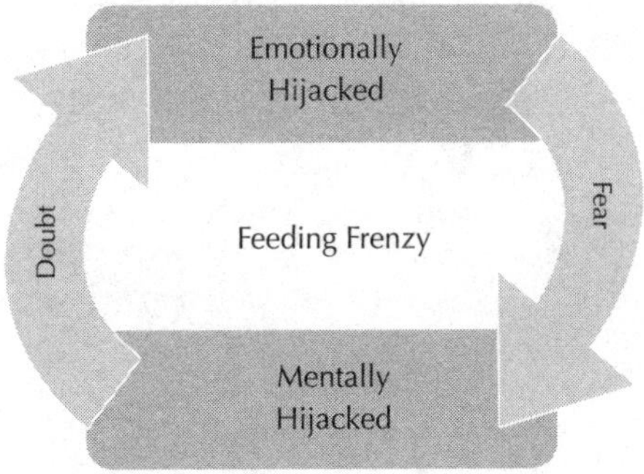

Figure 4

This incessant way of thinking mentally hijacks us, creating an inner state of doubt which, in turn, is fuelled by an intense emotional charge of fear that drives this uncomfortable state on and on. And we are seldom aware of it at the time. No matter how much we try to mask it, our voice, body language and behaviours broadcast our lack of confidence and our performance potential is severely compromised within this circumstantially dependent state.

**In Summary**

1. Adversity can evoke a *knee-jerk reaction* of fear and doubt, which hijacks our inner state.

2. A mentally and emotionally hijacked state undermines our capacity to think, feel and act appropriately.

3. Even when we try to mask our fear and doubt, our speech and behaviour inevitably give the game away.

## 6. A Facade of Pseudo-Confidence

In the real world adverse situations don't always let us off the hook. Sooner or later we have to pull ourselves up by our boot straps and face the unavoidable. At work and in our private lives as well, circumstances are such that we can only avoid threatening situations for so long.

> **Key Question:**
>
> When avoidance is no longer an option, what do you do to get yourself ready to face the unavoidable?

When faced with adversity, we so often *freeze* because our outer performance in speech and action is inhibited by the mental and emotional hijacking within us. This can occur for a split second, several minutes or even longer. Yet, the tendency to *freeze* is frequently our first port of call.

In these circumstances, what follows is either an avoidance strategy of *flight* or a more aggressive strategy of *fight*, in which we square up to the situation. Experience has taught me that the *freeze-flight* reaction does not always end there, and sooner or later ends up in a *fight* reaction, with the individual having to make a stand. As we have seen, life has a way of catching up with us and we can only avoid the inevitable for so long.

### Masking Our Fear and Doubt

When the *fight* reaction kicks in, in our desperation we often do all that we can to feel more confident and to have the impact we know is within our potential. In a confused and mentally or emotionally hijacked state we will make every effort to psyche ourselves up, drumming up the oomph to face the uncomfortable situation. When we attempt to mask our fear and doubt in order to project an air of confidence, what we end up with is a facade of pseudo-confidence – a mask that never lasts.

> 'If we attempt to mask our fear and doubt in order to project an air of confidence, what we end up with is a facade of pseudo-confidence – a mask that never lasts.'

The 'confidence' that follows is no more than a facade as it attempts to cover over or disguise our underlying fear and doubt. The fear and doubt do not really go away: they are only suppressed. The resulting projection of confidence is not the real deal, only a cover-up and pretence.

Some years ago I had the pleasure of working with Helen, a senior manager at a private bank. She disclosed, 'I psyche myself up.' She went on to say, 'I get exhausted – it really burns me up.' Because fear and doubt are suppressed, they constantly try to resurface and in these circumstances we have continually to create and re-create the facade and the suppression. It is like putting a ball under water: it will constantly try to resurface.

## Twin Processes of Projection and Suppression

Facade of Pseudo-Confidence

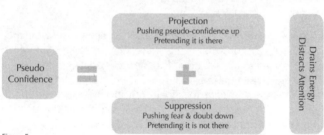

Figure 5

A facade of pseudo-confidence is directly dependent on the twin processes of projection and suppression (see Figure 5). In our desperation, we may do all that we can to project 'confidence' and suppress fear and doubt. However, the projection and suppression have to be continually sustained – and this drains our energy and depletes our potential impact relentlessly. It is neither a convincing nor a sustainable situation.

**In Summary**

1. In the Stretch Zone, we will have to face up to the situation sooner or later through a *fight* reaction.

2. When in an emotionally hijacked state, we tend to do all that we can to psyche ourselves up.

3. Fear and doubt do not go away – they are only suppressed.

4. Pseudo-confidence is a projection of 'confidence' over suppressed fear and doubt.

## 7. *Having* Confidence – A Desperate Strategy

When our inner state is mentally and emotionally hijacked within the Stretch Zone, the tendency is to do all that we can to *psyche ourselves* up and *convince ourselves* that we are confident, capable and worthy. What we are actually doing is attempting to superimpose a feeling of confidence over an underlying feeling of fear and doubt. Our hope in doing this is that we'll consequently *have* confidence and act accordingly.

---

**Key Question:**

What does *having confidence* mean to you and what is the effect of this on yourself in difficult situations?

---

The knee-jerk reaction of superimposing a projection of pseudo-confidence over suppressed fear and doubt can be described as the strategy of *having confidence*. The implication is that the confidence comes from the outside, rather than from within yourself. The superimposition is an add-on, an introduction of something that is assumed to be absent.

---

'The knee-jerk reaction of superimposing a projection of pseudo-confidence over suppressed fear and doubt can be described as the strategy of *having confidence*.'

---

Similar to the ways in which people attempt to boost their self-esteem by wearing branded clothing or driving a fancy car, the strategy of *having confidence* is about taking on something that makes us feel more confident. While driving a fancy car might make some of us feel good about ourselves, this is usually short-lived: as soon as someone else arrives in a better model the feel-good factor is soon gone, if it lasts that long in the first place.

### Thinkery-Thunkery

While you might attempt to have confidence through outer initiatives such as wearing a new suit, projecting your voice, adjusting your posture, writing down goals and the like, most of the having – the superimposition – happens internally, within the mind. *Having confidence* is a strategy that is characterised by a way of thinking whereby we try to convince ourselves of our confidence and potential.

> 'Having confidence is a strategy that is characterised by a way of thinking whereby we try to convince ourselves of our confidence and potential.'

The trouble is that it introduces a whole lot of additional 'thinking' to an already busy and uncertain mental state. What results is a battle between a 'positive' mode of thinking and 'negative' thinking. Donald Smith, a truly inspirational philosopher, referred to this as 'thinkery-thunkery', in which an already confused state is exacerbated by more confusion and, in our distraction, we end up walking, 'thunk', into a brick wall, doing or saying something that we otherwise would not have said or done.

On a good day, the two opposing forces battling within us tend to cancel each other out. Yet, all too often, the emotional charge and attachment driving the 'negative' mode of thinking tend to be so much more powerful than our puny attempts to keep a 'positive' train of thought. So 'positive' thinking soon gives way to 'negative' thinking and our feelings of inadequacy are exacerbated even further.

Even if the 'positive' thinking were to win the day, our *inner performance* is usually so distracted by all the thinking, effort and energy that goes into psyching ourselves up, that our outer performance reflects this distracted state and we perform below our maximum potential.

## Desperation Repels

The knee-jerk reaction to psyche ourselves up in the Stretch Zone is usually driven by the highly-charged emotional energy of desperation. This drive is so powerful that it further hijacks our faculties and incapacitates our *outer performance*. Yet the underlying attachment we all too often have to this emotional energy makes it difficult to observe it in play and even more difficult to let go of it when it really matters.

Some years ago I walked into my study and felt a spontaneous impulse to pick up a book on philosophy. I flicked it open to a random page and one phrase jumped out at me: *desperation repels*. It most certainly does. Whether in a sales situation, at an interview or on a date, when we sense that someone is desperate, this feeling becomes a serious turn-off which sets up barriers immediately.

Pseudo-confidence broadcasts our desperation. And no matter how we try to mask it, the harder we try to cover up our desperation with a veneer of pseudo-confidence, the more it will leak out in our mere presence, in our speech and actions.

## An Acquisitive Reaction

The paradigm or assumption underlying the strategy of *having confidence* is the idea that confidence is something that we somehow lack and need to acquire. Because of our conviction that we lack confidence, we do all that we can to acquire it and have it. What follows is a pretence that neither convinces nor lasts.

**In Summary**

1.   *Having confidence* superimposes a veneer of pseudo-confidence over fear and doubt.

2.   It is based on the assumption that confidence is something we lack and need to acquire.

3.   The superimposition takes the form of frenetic positive thinking to drown out negative thinking.

4.   The battle within impedes our *inner performance* and, as a result, our *outer performance*.

5.   Our desperation broadcasts our underlying inadequacy and uncertainty.

## 8. Spiral of Fear and Doubt

The strategy of *having confidence* never lasts; it is just not sustainable. Not only does it not last, it undermines the very confidence it is supposed to create, thereby inadvertently strengthening our feelings of insecurity and inadequacy. So how does this work?

> **Key Question:**
>
> In what ways might a facade of pseudo-confidence exacerbate your own feelings of inadequacy?

A house that is built on sand is just not going to endure: the cracks will quickly begin to show. In the same way, when we attempt to build up confidence on a foundation of fear and doubt, the 'confidence' that follows is just not going to sustain itself. In fact, it will take tremendous effort and energy to build in the first place and even more effort and energy to sustain it.

As we have seen, pseudo-confidence broadcasts desperation. And no matter how much we try to mask it, our desperation will be perceived by others.

Contrary to popular belief, our emotions are not as private as we might think. We continually infect each other emotionally, whether we intend to or not. We only have to spend time with someone who moans constantly to find that they soon infect us with their state. They don't even have to do or say anything specific: their mere presence will have its inevitable effect on us. Conversely, the same is true of someone who is upbeat and positive: their company is likely to lift us up. Our emotions are not private, but highly contagious and we infect each other constantly through our mere presence.

As a result of the highly-charged desperation underlying pseudo-confidence, we won't have to do or say anything concrete – our mere presence will convey our lack of confidence and people will respond to us accordingly.

## A Highly Dependent State

As we have seen, a veneer of pseudo-confidence is entirely dependent on the considerable effort and energy that goes into drumming up the oomph to face adversity. Having psyched ourselves up once will not make our newly found 'confidence' a permanent fixture. It needs to be constantly maintained. As soon as our efforts begin to dwindle, our feeling of confidence quickly fades too and our performance will drop accordingly.

To make matters even worse, as our confidence begins to wane, our emotional attachment to the idea that 'I am not a confident person' entrenches itself even more deeply, exacerbating our feelings of inadequacy. The mind very quickly uses this to justify the idea that 'I am not a confident person' and that 'I am justified in retreating within my comfort zone'.

Each time this happens, the result is a *spiral of fear and doubt*, in which one initial negative experience reinforces, entrenches and justifies the deeply-held conviction that 'I am not confident'. The emotional attachment to our unhelpful definitions of ourselves becomes stronger – and yet we seldom stop to question this.

**In Summary**

1. *Having confidence* and the facade that follows is just not sustainable.

2. A facade of pseudo-confidence actually exacerbates feelings of inadequacy.

3. The facade is directly dependent on the effort and energy needed to create and sustain it.

4. As the effort fades the facade drops – and fear and doubt resurface.

5. The resulting drop in confidence entrenches the conviction that: 'I am not confident.'

Part Two
# Scratching Below
# The Surface

## 9. Genuine Confidence

Your own observations in Chapters 1 and 4 will have shown you that your day-to-day experience is so often one of circumstantial confidence. When the situation is favourable most of us will feel confident. Yet when the circumstances are unfavourable, our confidence seems to disappear – and fear and doubt dominate our mentally and emotionally hijacked state.

> **Key Question:**
>
> How would you differentiate between genuine confidence and pseudo-confidence?

In the Stretch Zone we quickly start doing all we can to boost our confidence by psyching ourselves up, hoping to convince ourselves of our confidence and capability. The facade that follows is unconvincing and the cracks quickly begin to show.

Seldom pausing to question this repetitive process, we always do what we have always done and always get what we have always got. Einstein said that madness is to continue doing the same thing while hoping for a different result. In spite of past experiences in the Stretch Zone, we seem to hope against hope that our confidence will be there next time.

This type of wishful thinking is often fuelled by an endless stream of activities whereby we hope to acquire confidence. I came across a book that claims to offer 365 ways to develop confidence. However, what this book actually offers is a whole lot of different ways to create a facade of pseudo-confidence. This sort of 'confidence' just isn't going to last.

So we need to ask ourselves some questions. What is the alternative to pseudo-confidence? What needs to be known to realise this alternative? What misconceptions stop us from seeing this alternative? What do we mean by *genuine confidence*?

## Circumstantial Confidence

The difference between genuine confidence and pseudo-confidence rests on two fundamental distinctions.

---

### Example: Circumstantial Confidence

When I was coaching Jennifer, a senior manager at a bank in Ireland, she remarked that, 'I'm more vocal with people I know,' and qualified this with, 'in my own sphere of influence and subject matter.' Jennifer went on to say, 'I tend to get dumb struck when I'm not prepared.' Similarly, Marilouise commented that her confidence was dependent on 'having people respect or like me'.

Tanya described how: 'In certain situations I come across as confident, if comfortable with the people I am with.' Senior banker Andrew summed it up by saying, 'When I'm in an environment where I feel in control I can be extremely confident. When in an environment where I do not have control, my confidence can wane.'

---

These are certainly examples of circumstantial confidence. Jennifer's confidence is limited to the extent to which she feels her circumstances match her *preferences* for familiarity, subject knowledge and preparation. This – and I'm sure that Jennifer would agree – is a *self-imposed* limitation that is neither satisfactory nor fulfilling. A far more satisfying situation would be for her to feel free to make the impact she has the potential to make, anywhere, anytime.

## Real and Sustainable Confidence

Genuine confidence is a state that is independent of your circumstances and which comes from within yourself. Because it comes from within yourself, it is always there as a latent potential, anywhere, anytime. The differentiating factors are *independence* and *constancy*.

> 'Genuine confidence is a state that is independent of your circumstances and which comes from within yourself.'

A genuinely confident person would not lose her poise and composure, even if she found herself in a difficult situation. Her inner state would remain independent and constant, unmoved by the surrounding adverse circumstances, and she would simply engage with the situation and deal with things as they arose. While she might not feel very comfortable, she would not lose her composure and her capability and impact would reflect this.

Genuine confidence is authentic because it comes from within ourselves. It is sustainable because it is not dependent on any circumstances *without,* nor on activities that attempt to psyche ourselves up from *within*. Coming from within, genuine confidence is authentic and completely congruent with oneself.

**In Summary**

1.   Genuine confidence comes from within yourself and is completely congruent with who you already are.

2.   Coming from within, genuine confidence is *independent* of circumstance.

3.   Because it comes from within, genuine confidence is a *constant*, available to you anywhere, anytime.

## 10. Confidence: Our Day-to-Day Understanding

Given all that has been said, confidence appears to be an elusive concept. So how does it work? Why doesn't it always work when we need it most? How come it seems to work for us on some occasions, but not on others? When it isn't working, where does it go to? When it is working, where does it come from? And just why is it so difficult to switch it on when we need it most?

> **Key Question:**
>
> What does confidence mean to you?

'Confidence' is a familiar term which we use in everyday conversations. The impression is that we're all clear about what it means. When, however, we try to articulate our understanding, it soon becomes apparent that we are not as clear about it as we might previously have thought.

At least, this is what I have found in my work as a coach and facilitator. When people try to describe what they mean by confidence they mostly replace one concept with another, such as self-belief. You may have found something similar with the question above. This lack of clarity undermines our understanding and capacity for being confident in practice.

### What Everyday People Have Said

When coaching, another question I typically ask is: 'What does confidence mean to you?' The initial response is, more often than not, a pause, as people consider what they think and how to put their thoughts into words. When coaching Demi, a middle manager at a UK bank, it became clear to us both that in order to achieve her professional goals she needed to develop her confidence in her Stretch Zone. Her response to my question about confidence was to pause and then to reflect that, 'I'm not exactly sure.' Demi went on to say that confidence is 'when you believe in yourself that you can achieve what you want'. As her coach, my next question was, 'What does that tell you about confidence?'

Demi's view suggests that confidence requires self-belief – and it most certainly does. However, how do you go about developing self-belief? This is as much an enigma as developing confidence. While appreciating this problem is not to dismiss Demi's view – and her view is similar to that of most of us – it does challenge our thinking about the fundamental nature of confidence.

In response to the same question, Karen's response was, 'feeling comfortable in saying and doing what you want to in any situation'. What I like about Karen's view is that it implies confidence is an emotional state. What also appeals to me is that it refers to the freedom to do whatever we need to do in any given situation. This, in turn, implies freedom in speech and action without any self-imposed limitations. And yet instead we typically find that we feel constrained from responding spontaneously. We keep ourselves back, withholding our response or watering it down, changing it all together – or we do or say nothing at all. This view of confidence, however, does not tell us actually how *to be* confident.

## Misconceptions

While there is much to be taken away from Karen and Demi's descriptions, their views also highlight two key misconceptions about confidence which limit our understanding of it and application in practice. The two misconceptions are that confidence is about feeling *comfortable* and about achieving *results*. The next two chapters will explore these two misconceptions further.

### In Summary

1. While 'confidence' is a familiar term, we are not as clear about what it actually means as we might think.

2. We so often replace confidence with other terms such as 'self-belief', which does not help either.

3. Two misconceptions about confidence relate to the ideas of being *comfortable* and achieving *results*.

## 11. Comfort with Discomfort

Let's focus for a moment on Karen's description of confidence as 'feeling comfortable in saying and doing what you want to in any situation'. As we've seen, Karen introduces the idea of feeling comfortable in relation to confidence. At the heart of our day-to-day understanding is the idea that confidence and comfort somehow go hand-in-hand, that confident people feel comfortable in the Stretch Zone.

**Key Question:**

To what extent do confident people actually feel comfortable in the face of adversity?

When considering your answer to the above question, you may or may not be surprised to hear that the idea that confidence and comfort are inextricably linked is a fundamental misconception which actually undermines genuine confidence, impact and potential. In our misguided conviction that they go hand in hand, we end up spending a lot of time waiting around for that feeling of comfort to emerge, and, because we do not feel it, we withhold our natural spontaneity.

When describing confidence, Tanya said, 'Feeling comfortable goes hand-in-hand with confidence.' In today's demanding and ruthless world, we have such a powerful need to feel safe and secure – and this need all too often drives us to seek out our comfort zones, particularly whenever we feel exposed and vulnerable. With this comes the conviction that if we are confident we'll inevitably feel comfortable when in our Stretch Zone.

However, experience has taught me that, while confidence is linked to our emotional state, it is not dependent on our states of either comfort or discomfort. Confident people will often describe themselves as feeling far out of their comfort zones when engaged in difficult situations. So how do we make sense of this confidence vs. comfort dilemma?

## Performance Edge

In any high-performance situation, people who want to excel need to operate at their *performance edge*. This refers to that knife-edge of performance within the Stretch Zone, where we need to operate to our full potential without the luxury of reflection time, preparation or encouragement. One analogy is the experience of standing at the edge of a cliff: finding ourselves at our performance edge is likely to feel just as uncomfortable. One of our main misconceptions about confidence is that we believe we'll be able to face the Stretch Zone without that feeling of discomfort.

Operating at your performance edge and being in your comfort zone are mutually exclusive. Being on that edge necessarily requires you to come out of your comfort zone: until you do, you'll never be at your performance edge. Experience has taught me that confidence is never an issue when we find ourselves in our comfort zones. It only becomes an issue at the threshold of our Stretch Zones, wherever that might be.

> 'The idea of operating at your performance edge and being in your comfort zone are mutually exclusive.'

### Exercise: Blowing Up a Balloon

Blow up a balloon to its outmost potential, without having it burst in your face. The tension you feel when blowing up a balloon to its maximum capacity is akin to the discomfort you will feel at your performance edge. When we stretch ourselves at the performance edge we will feel a tension between exhilaration and fear. The fear is that, like the balloon, it might just backfire and burst in our face. The performance edge is the Stretch Zone and is simply not likely to feel like a very comfortable place to be.

## Comfort with Discomfort

Working with leaders over the years, I have found that high performers have an acceptance and tolerance for the discomfort that comes with being out of their comfort zones. I call it 'comfort with discomfort'. They remain focused on the performance and *not on their thoughts and feelings about the performance*. To hope that we'll be confident without feeling any discomfort is wishful thinking, an irrational self-limiting belief (see Figure 8).

> 'High performers have an *acceptance and tolerance* for the discomfort that comes with being out of their comfort zones.'

The alternative is to become mentally and emotionally hijacked and distracted by the negative thoughts and emotions that arise in the Stretch Zone. Rather than focus on the difficult situation itself, we then tend to focus on the fear and doubt, undermining our faculties in the process. Awareness and acceptance of discomfort are the means whereby we can free our inner faculties to focus where it matters most.

Confidence & Comfort

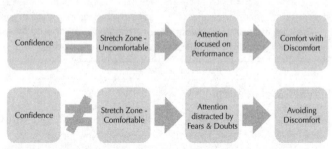

Figure 8

## Making it Look Easy

Richard, a senior manager, described confidence as 'being at ease with what you are talking about or doing'. Confident people seem to make facing difficult situations look easy. Well, that is how it looks from the outside. When discussing challenging situations with confident people, most will disclose that the situations were difficult and anything but easy. Yet from the outside, they made the situations look easy. Behind these outer appearances, their apparent ease usually relates more to their comfort with discomfort, their confidence and the situation itself, than with any sense of being unchallenged by the situation.

'When discussing challenging situations with confident people, most will disclose that the situations were difficult and anything but easy.'

Through their *comfort with discomfort,* confident people are able to avoid becoming distracted by their fears and doubts. Instead, they focus their attention on the difficult situation and behave accordingly.

## A Paradoxical Transition

Paradoxically, when in our discomfort we keep our nerve and face adversity with confidence, that initial discomfort often becomes less relevant and dissipates into thin air. So how does this work?

The discomfort only exists within our *private world*, our personal take on the situation and projection of our emotions and perceptions onto the *real world*. No one else knows about our discomfort. It is not a real feature of the challenging situation itself. It is something we create and project onto it. As we are the creators of the discomfort, it can only exist for as long as we continue to create it. As soon as our attention goes elsewhere, the discomfort disappears into the nothingness from which it came.

When we begin to master our confidence in the Stretch Zone and focus our attention where it really matters, this feeling of discomfort will diminish and we'll be able to engage with adversity without any discomfort whatsoever. However, until we pass through that transitional threshold, *comfort with discomfort* is the name of the game.

### In Summary

1.  A fundamental misconception is that confident people feel comfortable when facing adversity.

2.  The effect of this misconception is that many of us hold back our natural spontaneity until we feel comfortable in a challenging situation.

3. Our performance edge and comfort zones are mutually exclusive.

4. *Comfort with discomfort* helps confident people to focus on the difficult situation itself.

5. It means that we are not emotionally hijacked by our thoughts and feelings about our performance.

6. Paradoxically, when our attention goes to our actual performance our discomfort dissipates.

## 12. Confidence and Achieving Results

We saw in Chapter 10 how, when asked what confidence meant to her, Demi said it was 'when you believe in yourself that you can achieve what you want'. And we also learned how, in her description, Demi highlighted one of the most pervasive misconceptions we hold about confidence.

---

**Key Question:**

What has achieving results actually got to do with genuine confidence?

---

Perhaps the most incapacitating idea that undermines confidence is the assumption that confidence is about achieving results. In our results-obsessed world we have been force-fed a belief system of results and achievement. The importance of achievement is so entrenched in our psyches that we become champions of it whether we like it or not.

---

'Perhaps the most incapacitating idea that undermines confidence is the assumption that confidence is about achieving results.'

---

However, our fears and doubts are driven by the pressure, from both within and without, to achieve results. Consequently, we avoid our fear of failure by not stepping out of our comfort zones, in the belief that 'if I don't try I can't fail'. Thus we remain stuck in the realm of mediocrity and underachievement.

Achievement is not a bad thing of itself. In fact, it is a good thing and a vital element of human society. If granted disproportionate importance, however, the pressure to achieve will undermine us substantially. And most of the time it is way out of measure. And most of the time the pressure to achieve comes from within ourselves. While it might have its roots externally, what sustains it is our own conditioning, as we create and re-create it again and again. The effect is relentless.

## Results and Confidence

Dictionary.com defines confidence as a 'belief in oneself and one's powers or abilities'. So what does this tell us about confidence? While simply replacing the word 'confidence' with 'belief' is not that helpful, this definition actually sheds substantial insight on the nature of confidence – however, this is actually more in relation to what it does not say than what it does say. The key is to know what to look for.

What dictionary.com does not say is that confidence is about a belief in a certain outcome and about our powers and abilities to achieve that outcome. That is, confidence is not directly linked to the outcome, but is linked to our own faculties – our powers and abilities.

We have a range of powers and abilities – our inner faculties, which include mind, attention, reason, heart, perception and the like. Confidence is the ability to engage in the Stretch Zone with our inner faculties focused on the situation and not on securing a particular result.

My own experience suggests that we unintentionally undermine our confidence through our preoccupation with the results we crave. Rather than focus on the difficult situation itself, and on the application of our powers and abilities to it, we misdirect our attention to the outcome. Our preoccupation with the outcome distracts our inner faculties from the difficult situation and creates unnecessary pressure to achieve results.

What follows is a domino effect, which looks something like:

### Confidence and Results – A Domino Effect

1. Our attention becomes divided between the difficult situation and our desired result.

2. When this occurs, our capacity to attend to the difficult situation is diminished.

3. When this occurs, our ability to apply our powers and abilities is limited.

4.  When this occurs, our ability to perform to our potential is undermined.

5.  When this occurs, we realise that we are not going to achieve what we want to achieve.

6.  When this occurs, we become desperate – mentally and emotionally hijacked.

7.  And so we become further distracted, and our powers and abilities further undermined.

Following this repetitive pattern the situation snowballs: our inner state of readiness to engage in the Stretch Zone diminishes and with it our performance potential.

What makes our preferred outcome such a powerful distraction is our emotional attachment to whatever we want to achieve. When our desired outcome is under threat, our emotionally hijacked state undermines our *inner performance*, which has a direct and immediate impact on our *outer performance*.

### High-Control vs. Low-Control

Rather than focus on that which we stand a good chance of controlling – i.e. the application of our own powers and abilities – we tend to focus on what we can't control: the desired outcome. The effect on our performance potential is not very difficult to imagine. When we focus on an area of low-control we feel less certain, which in turn undermines our confidence, with detrimental consequences. While we might like to think that we can control the outcome, in reality the success or failure of this is usually related to many interdependent factors.

In fact, we'd do well to remember that the outcome has not actually happened yet and is only a *potential reality* sometime in the future. The only certainty is the *actual reality* in front of us in the present moment, in the form of our powers and abilities and the difficult situation. We should also be aware that the only way to impact on that *potential future reality* is by making an impact on the *actual present reality*.

While the result is some time in the future, the challenge that leads to the result is in the present. If we are preoccupied with the result itself, our inner faculties will be divided between the result in the future and the challenge in the present (see Figure 9). So long as our inner faculties remain divided and we fail to give our full attention to the challenging situation in the present, we will inadvertently undermine our capacity to perform with confidence and to our full potential.

Confidence & Results

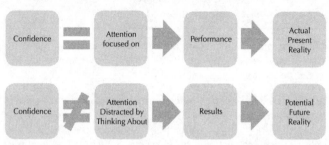

Figure 9

The present is the only moment that we can influence, the *moment-of-impact*. By influencing the present we stand a chance of making an impact on the future and future outcomes.

> 'Perhaps the most incapacitating idea that undermines confidence is the assumption that confidence is about achieving results.'

### Confidence and Interference

We know from experience that when we do not pay attention, we become ineffective and inefficient. With attention, both our performance and the odds of achieving our desired outcome improve substantially.

When we perceive our desired outcome to be under threat, the fear and doubt that follows become an interference that hijacks us mentally and emotionally and undermines our ability to attend to the difficult situation. However, as soon as we find the presence of mind to return our attention to the difficult situation itself, aligning our powers and abilities to it, a very different state arises – one full of potentiality.

The bottom line is that confidence is not so much about the outcome of the difficult situation and very much about the inner state of readiness to engage with it. Thinking about the performance and attending to the performance are two completely different things. The one is a distraction from the performance. The other is a conscious state of readiness to engage in the performance.

> 'Thinking about the performance and attending to the performance are two completely different things.'

### Example: Olympic Swimmer

In the moments before an event, an Olympic swimmer will focus on the present. He won't allow his attention to be swept away by distracting 'thoughts' about the result, about how good the other performers are, or whether he personally will be good enough. The swimmer has little or no control over those concerns. Instead, he focuses on the walk out to the arena, the walk towards the starting board, the look of the water, on being calm and composed – and all this occurs in the present, within that individual's control. When on the starting board, the athlete will not be thinking about the result; his attention is focused fully on the starting gun. If his mind is absent, thinking about the result, doubt is likely to creep in and compromise his performance.

Once the starting gun has fired, the swimmer's attention is on his dive technique and nothing else. During the swim his focus is on the stroke. And so the *moment-of-impact* changes as the event unfolds moment-by-moment. The present moment is where the Olympian focuses his attention and not on thoughts about the outcome.

> In a talk by Adrian Moorhouse, who won the Olympic gold for breast stroke in 1988, Adrian described how four years earlier, when he was favourite to win, he was struck by circling thoughts such as 'I can't win this', thinking of the result. And, in 1984, he didn't win: he came fourth.

It is important to emphasise, in no uncertain terms, that focusing on the present does not mean abandoning the goals towards which you are striving. This is certainly not the case. Any athlete will have clearly formulated goals towards which he or she is working. An athlete may even put her goals into writing, talking them through with her coach and continuously reformulate them in relation to her training and achievements. Goals are extremely helpful and provide a sense of purpose in our lives.

What is being described here is not the negation of goals, but the fact that athletes, for example, do not *think* about their goals or possible outcomes at the time of a performance. Instead, athletes focus on their stride, stroke or swing – on action in the Stretch Zone.

**Example: Katherine Jenkins**

When I was training a group of IT specialists in Cardiff, during the course of a discussion about leadership I discovered that two of the people in the group went to school with Katherine Jenkins, the opera singer. They both agreed that Katherine would never be swayed away from what she wanted to achieve. Her focus on her goal was said to be absolute.

I suspect that, when in her Stretch Zone performing on stage or in the studio, Katherine will not be thinking about her cheering fans – the result in the future. Instead she will be attending fully to the sound of her voice and the music in the present, as it sounds moment-by-moment, focusing on the *moment-of-impact*.

**In Summary**

1. Our greatest misconception is that confidence depends on the results we achieve.

2. This misconception has the effect of creating unnecessary pressure, which undermines our potential.

3. Confidence has nothing to do with results.

4. Confidence has everything to do with the alignment of our powers and abilities in the Stretch Zone.

5. The outcome is a *potential future reality*, an area of low-control that can elicit uncertainty.

6. Our powers and abilities are an *actual present reality*, an area of high-control.

7. A preoccupation with results creates an interference which mentally and emotionally hijacks our performance potential.

8. Thinking about our performance and attending to our performance are two different things.

9. Our emotional attachment to results makes it such a powerful form of interference.

## 13. Convicts of Our Own Convictions

Over the years it has become very apparent that confidence is often limited by several underlying misconceptions. If we poured our confidence in a bucket, each misconception would be like a big hole in that bucket, with our confidence draining out day after day.

---

**Key Questions:**

What misconceptions do you think society has about confidence? What misconceptions do you personally have about confidence?

---

The trouble with misconceptions is that we never think to question them. We simply assume that they are true. In fact, because we are so convinced of their validity, we are seldom, if ever, even aware of them in the first place. Because we are so convinced of what we think we know, we become convicts of our own convictions. In this way our misconceptions about confidence act as self-imposed limitations which hold us back and limit our potential.

---

'Because we are so convinced of what we think we know, we become convicts of our own convictions.'

---

### Fundamental Misconceptions about Confidence

As a coach and facilitator, I have come across a number of fundamental misconceptions about confidence. I have also found that we can overcome their limiting effects through understanding and awareness.

### 1. That the performance edge will feel comfortable

While it is easy to be confident in our comfort zones, it is not so easy to be confident in the Stretch Zone, which is always likely to feel uncomfortable. The consequence is that we procrastinate as we approach the performance edge, waiting to feel more comfortable before we proceed.

## 2. That undertaking challenging situations will eventually become easy

While confident people can make facing adversity look easy, this is not necessarily their experience. However, the misconception leads to our harbouring unrealistic expectations and waiting for the perfect moment to make a start.

## 3. That confidence is about achieving a result

When we place unmeasured emphasis on results we end up placing a lot of unnecessary pressure on ourselves, which distracts us from the very effort that is likely to deliver the result we desire. While confidence increases the likelihood of achievement, the confidence itself is neither defined nor dependent on the result.

### Example: Achieving Results

In a difficult situation – for example, one in which we did not succeed in achieving our goal – it would be unreasonable to conclude that because the results were not there, there was an absence of confidence. Confidence refers to our inner state. The results simply refer to the outcome of the effort. Confidence and results are two different things.

## 4. That confidence is something we lack

Believing that we lack confidence, we do all that we can to *have* and acquire it. We psyche ourselves up with confidence-boosting hype, which we superimpose over our suppressed fears and doubts. The result is a facade of pseudo-confidence that never lasts.

## 5. That lacking confidence is natural

Related to the last misconception is the conviction that a perceived lack of confidence is normal and natural. This is rooted in our day-to-day experience of ourselves – that 'I lack confidence' and 'so do those around me'. While lacking confidence might be common, this does not make it natural.

### 6. That confidence is the dominant, pushy stereotype

Dominant, pushy people seem to get what they want and are typically mistaken for being confident. Based on this idea, people try to emulate these behaviours, projecting an inauthentic and incongruent facade that just does not work.

A dominant, pushy facade is nothing more than a display of pseudo-confidence and is *circumstantially dependent*. As soon as a more dominant so-and-so comes along, the transition from top-dog to mutt happens in a fraction of a second and the pseudo-confidence disappears along with it.

> 'A dominant, pushy facade is nothing more than a display of pseudo-confidence and is *circumstantially dependent*.'

### 7. That confidence is only the domain of certain personalities

Related to the last concept is the conviction that confidence is limited to the lucky few by virtue of their personalities. Confidence is associated with being outspoken, loud and action-orientated – with the domain of the results-driven, task-focused extrovert. This excludes reflective, people-focused introverts.

The truth is that confidence is the domain of all personality types; it only looks and sounds different according to the individual. And difference does not imply absence.

### 8. That we are only of value when we are busy doing

We live in a world that is as obsessed with *doing* as it is with *achieving results*. The resulting misconception is that if we are not *doing* then we are of little value. With this misconception we constantly put ourselves under pressure to speak or act before we are ready. And when we do, the quality and impact of our performance is less than it might have been.

As soon as people recognise that confidence is as much about *non-doing*, inaction, as it is about *doing*, action, they give themselves permission to speak and act when they are good and ready. To pause before action is to increase your state of readiness before acting. Yet the pause is not an excuse to procrastinate. It is a measured moment of poise that precedes action, like a poised leopard ready to pounce.

### 9. That our feelings of confidence will be better tomorrow

Another idea is the notion that 'while I don't feel very confident today, I'll feel more confident tomorrow'. But procrastination drains our feelings of confidence. Confidence depends on our inner state and tomorrow is no guarantee of an improved state. Procrastinating in the deluded hope that we'll feel better tomorrow means putting our lives on hold unnecessarily.

As soon as we place these misconceptions under conscious observation, our paradigm shifts and they will consequently lose much of their hold on our confidence and performance potential.

---

**In Summary**

1. We are so often the convicts of our own self-imposed convictions.

2. These include the misconception that the performance edge will feel *comfortable*.

3. The mistaken belief that undertaking challenging situations will become *easy*.

4. The misguided notion that confidence is about achieving *results*.

5. The delusion that confidence is something we *lack*.

6. The faulty logic that lacking confidence is *natural*.

7. The misguided idea that confidence is the prerogative of the dominant, pushy *stereotype*.

8. The illusion that confidence is the domain of only *certain personalities*.

9. The incorrect conclusion that we are only of value when we are *busy doing*.

10. The unhelpful idea that our feelings of confidence will somehow be better *tomorrow*.

---

## 14. Professional Observations –The Good News

While the concepts of circumstantial confidence, pseudo-confidence and the like might sound like so much doom and gloom, nothing could be further from the truth. Just underlying this outer veneer is a world of confidence simply waiting to be discovered.

**Key Question:**

Given all that has been said, what is the good news underlying these observations and insights?

We are all, without exception, imminently confident beyond measure, anywhere, anytime. In order to release our inner confidence all we need to do is to create the conditions within which confidence is inevitable. Rather than trying to have confidence through performing 101 tricks of *confidence-boosting* hype, the only action we need to take is stop doing what does not work and start doing what does work. Nature will take care of the rest.

'We are all, without exception, imminently confident beyond measure, anywhere, anytime.'

### Professional Observations

Arising out of my professional practice over the years are a number of observations about confidence and our performance potential, which I'd like to share here. As you will see, we have discussed points 1 through to 13 already, so I'd like you to think of the first part of this list as a helpful reminder.

1.  Everyone experiences moments of both high and low confidence.

2.  Experiences of high or low confidence are often circumstantially dependent.

3.  The circumstances that enable or disable confidence are different for different people.

4. Seemingly confident people desire to develop confidence as much as those who seem less confident.

5. Low confidence is always accompanied by a mentally and emotionally-hijacked state of fear and doubt.

6. No one ever intentionally decides to doubt himself: doubt is a conditioned habit.

7. The fear that accompanies low confidence is dependent on the conditioned doubt.

8. People attempt all sorts of ways to psyche themselves up with confidence boosting hype.

9. The confidence that follows from psyching ourselves up is a facade of pseudo-confidence which is not sustainable.

10. With pseudo-confidence, fear and doubt are suppressed but do not go away.

11. Sustaining the projection of pseudo-confidence and suppression of fear and doubt burns energy and distracts us mentally.

12. Because it is a facade, pseudo-confidence actually exacerbates fear and doubt.

13. Confidence has nothing to do with results; it is a *state of readiness* to perform to our potential.

While the observations outlined above relate to what we have already covered previously, the following observations relate to aspects that will be covered in the remaining chapters.

1. Confidence manifests naturally and effortlessly for all of us under certain conditions.

2. Once we have addressed our conditioned doubt, genuine confidence surfaces naturally from within.

3. Conditioned doubt is a self-imposed limitation: it's our own creation that no one else knows about.

4. Because we continuously create and re-create that doubt, we can simply 'un-create' it.

5. Un-creating conditioned doubt requires a conscious choice.

6. Making a conscious choice requires us to come out of our state of autopilot, within which doubt thrives.

7. Once the conditioned doubt is removed, the fear goes and confidence manifests naturally.

8. Confidence is an innate potential for everyone, regardless of personality or experience.

---

**In Summary**

1. Our ability to observe the facade of pseudo-confidence is actually very *good news*.

2. Just below this veneer is a *reservoir of confidence* waiting to be discovered.

3. Genuine confidence requires a paradigm shift and a change in our inner state.

---

## 15. So What Actually is Confidence?

So far we have asked lots of questions about confidence and reflected on a number of observations drawn from our day-to-day experience. At this stage we have most probably raised more questions than we've yet found answers for. So what actually is confidence after all?

---

**Key Question:**

Given what we've covered so far, how would you define confidence now?

---

Definitions can be useful in that they enable clarity in our understanding, observation and conversation. They can, however, narrow our thinking and perceptions too. As soon as we think we know something we tend to stop seeing it for what it is and only see our ideas about it.

---

'As soon as we think we know something we tend to stop seeing it for what it is and only see our ideas about it.'

---

I'd like to stress that the definition of confidence presented here is only intended to be a starting point and not a conclusion. We need to come to our own understanding individually and that is something that we can only do for ourselves. And the best way is through direct observation and experience.

---

**Confidence is an inner state of certainty that I can perform to my potential and deal with things as they arise, fearlessly and without caution or hesitation, free from any inner or outer limitations.**

---

***Inner State:*** confidence is a state and not a skill. A skill is something we can acquire, such as the ability to stimulate conversation through open questions, or jump over hurdles while sprinting flat out, or manage our emotions, or think creatively or to visualise a building that is yet to take physical form. A state is the inner platform or structure upon which our skills depend.

A state refers to our inner condition: our mind, heart, perception, identity, reason, attention and the like. Confidence is a state that arises when our inner faculties are aligned to create a firm foundation upon which our performance is based, regardless of circumstance. When our faculties are aligned, confidence arises naturally. However, like a skill, this state can be learnt and developed through knowledge, awareness and practise.

As a state, confidence is not so much about doing something, as being something. It is a state of being, not a state of doing. In the Stretch Zone we do not need to do anything to be confident, we only have to be. Within this state of being, our inner faculties align and function effectively according to their nature and our confidence and performance potential follow naturally.

> 'As a state, confidence is not so much about doing something, as being something.'

**Certainty:** confidence is about *being* self-assured: it's about the sense of certainty that comes from within, not from outside dependencies. With certainty comes calm composure, even in the Stretch Zone. This composure does not imply we are in our comfort zone. It means that we are comfortable with the discomfort and are able to *deal with things as they arise*.

> 'With certainty comes calm composure, even under pressure.'

What certainty does not imply is arrogance. Arrogance and confidence are two very different things; the difference becomes screamingly obvious when you consider the impact these very different states have on others. While arrogance creates dissonance and puts people off, confidence creates resonance and inspires.

**Perform to my Potential:** as soon as our inner performance is no longer disabled by a mentally and emotionally hijacked state of fear and doubt, our outer performance responds accordingly. Performing to our potential implies that we are already in a heightened *state of readiness* to do so.

> 'If we don't step up we'll never discover our limits and capabilities.'

Performing to our potential does not mean that everything will go the way we want or that we'll achieve things left, right and centre. Confidence is neither about unrealistic expectations nor results. It is about performing to your potential without any self-imposed limit.

Performing to your potential implies a willingness to step up and take a risk to test yourself against your potential. If you don't step up into your Stretch Zone you'll never discover your limits and capabilities.

**Deal with Things as They Arise:** confidence only becomes an issue when it is absent – however, it is usually absent when there is uncertainty or various unknowns about situations, outcomes and people. Life is certainly full of uncertainties and if it wasn't it would be pretty dull and boring. Confidence in the Stretch Zone is an inner state of certainty that we can deal with these unknowns in accordance with our potential as and when they arise.

The alternative is fear and doubt as we withdraw within our comfort zone, where there are fewer unknowns. Confidence is the willingness to get out of our comfort zone, engage and see what happens when we do, with the certainty that we'll be able to *deal with things as they arise*.

**Fearlessly:** in 1933 President Franklin D. Roosevelt said 'all we have to fear is fear itself'. When we look at little children, depending on their life experience, they fear nothing. They are generally fearless. In contrast to the distant memory of this childlike state, we, as adults, have often learnt to fear this or fear that. Our fear becomes an entrenched and conditioned behaviour – and its effect is relentless.

> 'All we have to fear is fear itself.' - Franklin D. Roosevelt

Genuine confidence does not mean that there is an absence of fear, as fear can be a very natural response to certain situations. However, confidence simply means that we are not incapacitated by imaginary fears. We are aware of the fear and see it as an emotion that will pass like every other emotion in recorded history. In a state of fearlessness we are able to function effectively with our inner faculties intact, free from distraction.

To fear nothing is freedom – and the greatest freedom is that which we possess within ourselves when we are free from our self-imposed limitations. Nelson Mandela, in his famous speech in which he quoted Marianne Williamson, said that 'our deepest fear is that we are powerful beyond measure'. To master fear in the Stretch Zone is to master yourself in that zone and, in so doing, to release your power and confidence 'beyond measure'. Marsilio Ficino, the renaissance philosopher, said 'he who does not master himself is master of nothing'.

**Without Caution or Hesitation:** when we are in the grip of fear and doubt, caution and hesitation follow as unwanted shadows. With fear and doubt we withdraw into our comfort zones so as to avoid having to deal with things as they arise. We might hesitate out of fear of failure, of being laughed at, of not knowing, fear of looking the fool, being disliked and so on.

If we are in the grip of caution and hesitation our inner performance is usually dominated by *analysis-paralysis*, where we do a lot of 'thinking' and over-analysis about what we're going to do or say next and how people might respond. The bulk of this pseudo-thinking is a very mindless, repetitive, negative train of thought which is preoccupied with what has happened in the past and what might happen in the future, rather than what is really going on in the present.

This mental hijacking serves no purpose other than to *distract focus* and *detract potential*. We never intentionally choose to 'think' these thoughts. They simply come through conditioned habit. I'm not sure that I have ever heard someone say that they deliberately chose to doubt themselves. Siofra, an award-winning leader working in banking, summed this up, saying that it is about 'trusting my instinct more, not having to think it through'. This is the difference between being a *warrior* and a *worrier*.

It is important to emphasise that I'm by no means suggesting *reflection and consideration* are not helpful, or that we need to act or speak immediately, impulsively. Some people have a natural disposition to *look before they leap* – and others just leap. Neither of these two styles is better than the other. Reflection can be a very powerful thing. The key is *measure*. While some reflection can be helpful, incessant *analysis-paralysis* at the threshold of the Stretch Zone is usually not and is typically merely a conditioned habit, an avoidance strategy.

***Free from Any Inner or Outer Limitations:*** in order to discover our inner reservoir of confidence in the Stretch Zone, we need to break free from the limitations that bind us. While some limitations are imposed externally, most limitations come from within. We are so often our own worst enemies, holding ourselves back unnecessarily.

While the descriptions of genuine confidence as outlined above might not be exhaustive, they certainly direct application in practice. It offers an *inspirational ideal* towards which to strive. Each time we act with confidence, in that moment we have achieved the ideal. Confidence is not some way-out impossibility that is seldom achieved, but an everyday occurrence that is more familiar than we might think.

The more often that these insights are digested and practised, the more familiar they will become, until they become *second nature* to us. Until then, I'd recommend that you avoid self-criticism whenever you achieve less than the ideal. Rather than dismiss your successes, even the little ones, you need to acknowledge them as a step in the right direction.

**In Summary**

1. When we think we know something we often stop seeing it and only perceive our idea about it.

2. As a state, confidence is not about *doing* something, but about *being* something.

3. Confidence is about *being* certain, with calm composure and self-assuredness.

4. Confidence is a heightened *state of readiness* to perform to our potential.

5. Confidence begins with *stepping up* and dealing with unknowns as they arise.

6. Confidence is not an absence of fear, but the capacity to focus on the task in hand and not the fear relating to it.

7. Confidence is an absence of the unmeasured caution whereby we become mentally hijacked by analysis paralysis.

8. Confidence is about being free from your self-imposed limitations, within and without.

## Part Three
# The First Principle

### 16. *Principle One*: Confidence as the Absence of Doubt

Years ago, when the issue of confidence came up during a coaching conversation with a financial services manager in the UK, I asked him what confidence meant to him. Practising self-observation, I heard the question being asked and noticed an immediate response arise within myself. The simplicity of the response and the implications of it were immediately apparent. My observation was that *confidence is the absence of doubt.*

---

**Key Question:**

What does *confidence as the absence of doubt* mean to you?

---

Following that conversation I spent some time contemplating the observation. What does the statement really mean? What is its practical value? To what extent is it actually true? If confidence is the absence of doubt, how do we get rid of doubt? What is doubt and where does it come from? When there is an absence of doubt, where does it go to? How does the doubt come and go? Who doubts and who is affected by doubt? Who decides to do the doubting in the first place? To what extent are we aware of doubt at the time? (See Figure 11.)

Confidence as the Absence of Doubt

Figure 11

When we lack confidence and cautiously hold ourselves back, there is inevitably a lot of doubt in our mind. In contrast, when we are full of confidence, there is an absence of doubt and we respond with natural spontaneity. When we are full of confidence there is an absence of doubt. When we lack confidence there is a profusion of doubt. What could be simpler than that? Hearing this for the first time, Martin, a senior bank manager, said, 'That's right… it just sums it up.'

> 'When full of confidence there is an absence of doubt. When we lack confidence there is a profusion of doubt.'

While confidence is difficult to define in itself, it is relatively easy to identify what it is not, and that is doubt. Having identified what something is not, i.e. its direct opposite, all we need to do is eliminate that opposite and what remains is what we're attempting to understand (see Figure 12).

Confidence as the Absence of Doubt

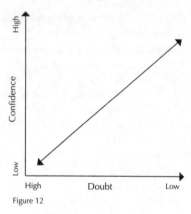

Figure 12

Demi described confidence as 'when you stop worrying about what people think about you' and went on to say that it is 'when you stop your fear of failure'. Both these descriptions correspond directly to confidence as the absence of doubt. Marilouise described her own situation: 'Externally I give off the impression [of confidence]; internally I'm like, oh my God, what is going on here.' What Marilouise recognised was that, while we might project a facade of confidence on the *outside*, frequently there is a profusion of doubt going on in the *inside*.

## Confidence vs. Doubt

Another way to describe the relationship between confidence and doubt is to say that they are *mutually exclusive*, where one is inversely proportionate to the other.

Confidence and doubt are, however, not a matter of absolute, 'either/or' alternatives, like a switch that is either 'on' or 'off'. They are rather a matter of degree, with many levels in-between the two extremes. Following this analogy, they are more like a dial that can be turned up or down, with many options between 'on' or 'off'.

The beauty of the principle is that it is not only self-evident; it is also memorable and practical: confidence as the absence of doubt directs effort and energy to where it matters most.

---

**In Summary**

1. Confidence is the *absence of doubt*.

2. When we are full of confidence, there is an absence of doubt.

3. When we are full of doubt, there is an absence of confidence.

4. Confidence and doubt are *mutually exclusive*.

---

## 17. Circumstantial Confidence and the Absence of Doubt

Due to the utter simplicity of the principle, describing confidence as the absence of doubt has proved to be of immense practical value in a coaching and facilitation context. It is direct, concise and memorable. The truth of it is also immediately apparent.

On hearing the principle, my coaching client Helen commented, 'Yeah, that's spot on; that is what people tell me – I should stop doubting myself.' In fact, you might easily argue that it is nothing other than common sense, and you would be right. Sue Warman, a friend and colleague, put it very nicely, observing, 'While it might be *common sense*, it is not necessarily *common practice*.'

> 'While it might be common sense, it is not necessarily common practice.'
>
> Sue Warman

Someone once said, 'The obscure we see eventually; the immediately apparent takes a little longer.' We are so conditioned to expect complex solutions to complex problems that we struggle to see the simplicity of what is right in front of us.

> 'The obscure we see eventually; the immediately apparent takes a little longer.'
>
> Unknown

> **Key Question:**
>
> What does circumstantial confidence have to do with confidence as the absence of doubt?

As mentioned previously, our day-to-day experience is that of circumstantial confidence, where our confidence comes and goes depending on our circumstances. This yo-yo experience of confidence is very much related to confidence as the absence of doubt.

## Circumstantial Confidence – A Game of Substitution

Circumstantial confidence is directly related to the relationship between confidence and doubt. Because confidence and doubt are mutually exclusive, they are continually coming and going, with one substituting the other in a seemingly never-ending cycle – depending on our *perception* of our circumstances at the time. Confidence and doubt seem to play a game of substitution, not because of conscious choice on our part, but through our conditioned perception (see Figure 14).

Doubt & Circumstantial Confidence

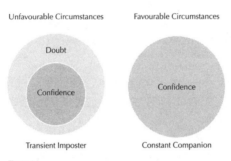

Figure 14

---

**Example: Taking a Penalty**

When coaching Duncan, a junior manager, he described a recent experience where, at a corporate league football match, he was required to take a penalty. This was his first penalty in quite a while. He missed and felt less than happy about it. Duncan described how, in a subsequent game, he found himself back in the Stretch Zone, having to take another penalty. He missed again.

He described how his thoughts were preoccupied with the previous miss. Doubt about what happened in the past and what might happen in the future undermined his confidence and capability in the Stretch Zone at the *moment-of-impact*.

A really important observation is to recognise that it is not confidence that comes and goes, but doubt – depending on our perception of the situation within the Stretch Zone. It might seem like it is our confidence that comes and goes, but that is only an appearance. Confidence is a constant companion, whereas doubt is a transitory impostor. We'll return to this in a later chapter as it plays such an important role in understanding the nature and substance of confidence in practice.

'Confidence is a constant companion, whereas doubt is a transitory impostor.'

**In Summary**

1. While confidence as the absence of doubt might be *common sense*, it is not *common practice*.

2. Confidence and doubt play a repetitive game of substitution, with one replacing the other.

3. Confidence is a *constant companion*, whereas doubt is the *transitory impostor*.

## 18. Doubt – *What* vs. *That*

To understand confidence as the absence of doubt more fully, we need to refine our understanding of the nature of doubt. To begin with, we need to understand an important distinction between *what* we doubt as opposed to *that* we doubt.

---

**Key Question:**

In releasing confidence, which is more important, knowing *what* we doubt or being aware *that* we doubt it?

---

When coaching, I have found that people quickly accept the principle that confidence is the absence of doubt and immediately begin to disclose *what* it is they doubt. This is driven by the Western conviction that as soon as we can identity *what* we doubt and *why* we doubt it, our doubts will be resolved, problem sorted!

On hearing the principle, Jenny said she doubts along the lines of: 'How people will see me, what will they think?' Tanya described her doubts too: 'What am I going to say next? Am I going to say something stupid?' There is a widely-held idea that if we identify what we doubt and why we doubt ourselves in this way, this process will somehow free us from the limiting impact of our doubt.

### Nothing Really New

Whether it is about our ability, our achievements, what others think, feeling accepted, being liked, our knowledge, our experience or our capacity to express ourselves, most of us are able to identify our doubts in the Stretch Zone very quickly. The question is to what extent is this useful in practice?

The most common reason why we can identify our doubts so quickly is that we know what they are in the first place. Discovering what we doubt is usually not a major light-bulb moment. However, naturally this is not always the case and at times people will discover something new. By and large, though, we have a good sense of what it is that bothers us.

### *That* We Doubt

Having identified *what* it is we doubt about ourselves, the question arises as to the effect this has on our performance potential. The effect is, at best, limited. While we might know *what* we doubt, we still have to deal with *the act of doubting* itself.

If identifying what we doubt – the *content* of our doubts – was the key, most of us would have moved on to greater confidence a long time ago. Yet why, when we have this knowledge, do we continue to experience diminished confidence?

When we say that confidence is the absence of doubt we are not saying that confidence is the absence of *this* doubt or *that* doubt. It is simply the absence of doubt. It really does not matter *what* you doubt. What matters is *that* you doubt it. Knowledge about the *content* (the 'what') is secondary to awareness of the *process* (the 'that') of doubting yourself (see Figure 15).

Doubt - What vs. That

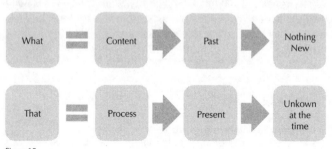

Figure 15

### *Why* We Doubt

Travelling from a sales meeting in Brussels, I fell into conversation with the CEO of a leading edge consultancy about the basic premise underlying this book. While accepting the idea that confidence is the absence of doubt, this individual was adamant that we not only have to identify *what* we doubt, but also *why* we doubt it – the root cause. This Western, psychodynamic idea suggests that an increased understanding and acceptance of the cause would have a cathartic effect, freeing us to move on to greater confidence.

While a greater understanding of what causes us to doubt can help, the question arises as to how feasible achieving this level of understanding is in our day-to-day lives. Given the complexities of our lives, the probability of our finding the root cause, assuming there is a single root cause, is not that great. And, even if we did, we would still have to deal with the effects of our conditioned behaviour in the Stretch Zone, when it really matters.

Another concern is that this may potentially lead to a *victim mentality*. The circumstances out of which our doubt originally sprang will inevitably have involved significant people and events in our lives. A victim mentality can seduce us into blaming our inadequacy on others, thereby creating a situation that makes moving on next to impossible. So long as we avoid taking responsibility for our responses to life, our capacity to move on will be dramatically undermined.

While our doubt might have begun with a particular event or relationship in the past, ten or twenty years later it is we ourselves who continue to create and re-create that doubt – no one else. Doubt is a self-imposed limitation which we inflict on ourselves at the threshold of the Stretch Zone. Playing the victim is an indulgence that is just not in our best interests, excusing us from being accountable or moving on responsibly.

---

**Example: Throwing a Strop!**

Someone who tends to throw a strop when they do not get their way might discover that the cause of this behaviour pattern is that Mum did the same in their formative years. Regardless of this knowledge, they will nonetheless still have to learn to deal with the actuality of the conditioned behaviour at the moment-of-impact.

---

This is certainly not to dismiss the value of knowing the *content* (the 'what') of our doubt, which can help us to recognise it as it arises in the mind. Its impact, however, is limited and can only take us so far. In the Stretch Zone we have to deal with the *process* (the 'that') of doubting ourselves, the activity at the *moment-of-impact*. Confidence is undermined by the process of doubting, not the content of the doubt.

> **In Summary**
>
> 1. To understand doubt we need to distinguish between *what* we doubt and *that* we doubt.
>
> 2. Most people know what they doubt about themselves but the effect of this knowledge is marginal.
>
> 3. While we might know what we doubt, we still have to deal with the doubt itself.

## 19. Doubt – Knowledge vs. Awareness

When looking at confidence as the absence of doubt, we need to make another important distinction – and that is between *knowledge* and *awareness*. While knowledge and awareness are both important, we tend to misunderstand the distinction between the two and their impact in the Stretch zone.

**Key Question:**

How would you differentiate between knowledge and awareness?

Working in the learning and development industry, I have found over the years that knowledge and awareness are often viewed as being completely synonymous. And this is not only the case with trainees, but also with many of the consultants who do the training. The assumption is that if we know something then we are aware of it. Conversely, if we are aware of something then we must know about it. The association between knowledge and awareness, as described here, would take some arguing to discount. The conclusion is that knowledge and awareness are one and the same thing.

Viewing knowledge and awareness as synonymous is, however, a limiting misconception which has significant implications for confidence in the Stretch Zone. It is like doing surgery with a hacksaw. The distinction is best explored by way of an example.

**Example: Feedback on Behaviour**

A manager receives feedback that he is abrupt and confrontational. Having received the feedback, we could say that he now has *knowledge* about the behaviour. We could also argue that he is now *aware* of the behaviour, which he was not aware of before. At this point knowledge and awareness seem to be the same thing. However, as soon as we explore the example a bit more, it quickly becomes apparent that the two concepts are not the same.

When the next frustrating situation arises, a situation that typically provokes an abrupt response from the manager, the question we need to ask is to what extent is he *aware of his behaviour at that particular moment*? While he might have the knowledge, this does not mean he is aware of it at the time.

If aware, he can choose whether to behave abruptly or not. If unaware, he is likely to do what he has always done – and get what he has always got.

This important distinction highlights the extent to which we are *aware* of our behaviour at the *moment-of-impact*. In the case of the manager in the example, *knowing* about abruptness is not enough. Knowledge of his abruptness is *necessary but not sufficient*.

Let us say that the manager has another abrupt episode and a colleague asks him about it afterwards. It would be highly likely that he would be able to describe his behaviour. That is, he has the retrospective *knowledge*, but not the immediate *awareness*. So what does this have to do with confidence in the Stretch Zone?

Just as changing behaviour such as abruptness requires both knowledge and awareness, so changing a conditioned habit such as doubt requires both too. It is simply not sufficient for us *to know* that we doubt ourselves, albeit with knowledge of both the *process* and the *content* of our doubt. We need to be aware of our doubt in the present moment, in the Stretch Zone, at the *moment-of-impact*. If we are not aware of it in that moment, it is highly unlikely that we'll be able to do anything about it.

### In Summary

1. Although often viewed as synonymous, knowledge and awareness are not the same thing.

2. Knowledge about behaviour does not imply awareness of it at the *moment-of-impact*.

3. Knowledge of the doubt is necessary but not sufficient – we need to be *aware* of it too.

## 20. Doubt – Helpful vs. Harmful

Another perspective from which to deepen our understanding of doubt is the possibility that there might be some value in it. To what extent might doubt be a good thing that adds value? Is doubt necessarily bad? In what way might doubt be helpful?

**Key Question:**

From your experience, in what way might doubt be helpful?

In his poem 'If', Rudyard Kipling writes: 'If you can trust yourself when all men doubt you, But make allowance for their doubting too'. Here, Kipling seems to suggest that we keep an open mind, a key characteristic of confidence.

### Positive and Negative Doubt

Negative doubt refers to that mindless, pseudo-thinking that arises as if out of nowhere. It is about *imaginary unknowns* concerning what has happened in the past and what might happen in the future. The critical factor is that we are hardly aware of it at the time. Yet, while we might not be aware of it, its impact in the Stretch Zone is relentless. Doubt, in this sense, arises out of conditioned habit and not from conscious choice. It is entirely irrational and is driven by the fear that accompanies it.

Positive doubt is something quite different. We might, for example, realise that we are simply out of our depth. Whereas irrational doubt is about *imaginary unknowns* that have no reality in the present, positive doubt is a more rational form of doubt which arises in response to the actualities of what is taking place in the real world. So to what extent might this form of doubt be helpful?

'Irrational doubt is about imaginary unknowns that have no reality in the present.'

**Arrogance vs. Humility**

Where there is a complete absence of positive doubt *arrogance* is likely to follow. We become overly confident, too sure of ourselves. When I was coaching Helen, she expressed a concern 'about the dividing line between confidence and arrogance'.

Arrogance is when people believe in their own hype. They are so convinced of their importance that they become convicts *of their own conviction*, trapped in their viewpoint. There is pride, haughtiness and conceit. Arrogance brings with it a feeling of superiority – 'being better than'. This is not confidence.

Confidence is characterised by *humility*, a humble attitude – and an unassuming stance. To assume something is to think we know, and as soon as we think, 'I know', we switch off to further enquiry. Assumptions are based on past knowledge, not the *special knowledge* of the present. To engage in that special knowledge we need to be open to the present, with an unassuming outlook.

So to what extent is humility synonymous with doubt? I would suggest that these are two very different concepts. Doubt implies boundless caution that limits spontaneity. Humility does not imply the fear associated with the unknown. To be humble is not to be full of fear. It is to be aware that we are not all knowing. To be humble is to be modest and unassuming. We can be very *certain about ourselves and yet filled with humility* at one and the same time. Mahatma Gandhi is an outstanding example.

> 'We can be very certain about ourselves and yet filled with humility at one and the same time.'

So what does this mean in practice?

**Absence of Doubt and Presence of Humility**

Viewing confidence as the absence of doubt is not to dismiss *rational* or *positive* doubt out of arrogance. Rather, as we have seen, genuine confidence is characterised by humility, an unassuming quality that is open to the views of others and the possibility that we might not be all-knowing and right. Indeed, with humility comes confidence, whereas arrogance can lead to alienation and to a loss of confidence.

Arrogant people often project an air of self-importance that dismisses others. This habit creates a position of high-exposure from which they are likely to fall. When we are arrogant, the assumption that we are important and capable of making an impact can cut us off from reality *as it is:* we inadvertently place ourselves on a pedestal from which we are likely to fall. Lurking behind a facade of arrogance is a conscious or unconscious insecurity which undermines the very confidence we are attempting to project. Arrogance is, at best, no more than a facade of *pseudo-confidence*.

Confidence with humility is easier to handle. There is no pedestal from which to fall. There is less pressure to be better than others. The ability to accept and acknowledge our fallibility implies confidence in and of itself. In the Stretch Zone, confidence is not only the absence of doubt; it is also the presence of humility.

**In Summary**

1. A complete absence of positive doubt can lead to arrogance.

2. Arrogance is nothing more than a facade of pseudo-confidence.

3. Positive doubt is about rational observations in the real world.

4. Negative doubt is about conditioned, irrational pseudo-thinking.

5. Confidence is very much about the qualities of humility and an unassuming outlook.

## 21. Opportunities Don't Come and Stay

Irrespective of the context, whenever we are in the Stretch Zone and caught up in a world of doubt, caution and hesitation will follow as a frustratingly persistent shadow. As opportunities come, our doubt compels us to hold ourselves back unnecessarily.

---

**Key Question:**

Referring back to the exercise in Chapter 1, in what situations does your spontaneity nosedive?

---

When we hold ourselves back unnecessarily, we quickly become frustrated with ourselves in the belief that we have let ourselves down. And no matter how much we attempt to justify or mask it, the frustration builds with self-criticism and self-recriminations that only exacerbate our mentally and emotionally hijacked state.

---

**Example: Holding Back**

Whenever I'm facilitating I've found there'll always be quiet people in the group. Yet whenever they say something it is usually well worth hearing. As a facilitator I make a point of discussing this with them and what often emerges is a highly repetitive pattern for them.

They will be sitting in the group, taking in the facilitated conversation. At some stage a thought will come to mind. Rather than share it, fear and doubt hijack them and they hold themselves back. Their mental state will be dominated by a mountain of 'thinking' – and doubt.

These people doubt the value of their observations. They worry about how the others might respond, or that they'll look foolish, or whether they'll make sense and so on. This pseudo-thinking centres on what has happened in the past and what might happen in the future. I call it *analysis-paralysis*.

---

> They will either hold themselves back completely, saying nothing at all, or, having perfected the response, they will share it after some time. The group and the conversation have, however, moved on and the contribution evokes the feeling of, '*Hello*, we moved on a while ago!'

This pattern is very common and can dominate our contribution to life. However, we are mostly unaware of it and the analysis-paralysis that goes with it at the time. When our inner performance is undermined, the effect on our outer performance is direct and immediate.

## Natural Spontaneity

When defining confidence, senior manager Helen described it as 'being yourself' and 'being able to show your true person'. This insightful observation highlights our very human need to be natural and spontaneous. When we hold back our natural spontaneity, we undermine our spirit and humanity; we cover ourselves over with a veil that shrouds our inner Self.

This is so obvious in little children. They fear nothing and respond naturally and spontaneously, without any self-imposed fears or doubts. Most children are the same on the outside as they are on the inside. They are true to themselves. They are authentic and congruent.

As adults bruised by life's knocks and bumps, we filter our natural spontaneity in the deluded hope that we'll be able to protect ourselves from further bumps. What we end up with is a situation where who and what we are on the inside is so different to who and what we are on the outside. We become inauthentic and incongruent, unhappy and unfulfilled.

Genuine confidence is about re-discovering our natural spontaneity and responding to situations as and when they arise – free from self-imposed fear and doubt.

## Nature of Opportunities

Of one thing we can be certain: opportunities don't come and stay; they come and go. The window of opportunity is defined –

that is why it is called a window. When we hold ourselves back we are in danger of missing the moment and opportunities will pass us by.

> 'Of one thing we can be certain: opportunities don't come and stay; they come and go.'

The good news is that when we take advantage of opportunities, circumstances have a way of developing in unexpected ways to support us in our choices. When we *step up* in the Stretch Zone we find that we have everything within our power to meet the situation and *deal with things as they arise*.

Another bit of good news is that opportunities are like waves on the beach. There is never only the one wave, but a continual process in which one wave is followed by another. So if you've missed an opportunity, get out of your mentally hijacked state as another opportunity is bound to be following close behind. Be there, be present and meet the next opportunity as it comes.

**In Summary**

1. Opportunities don't come and stay; they come and go.

2. With fear and doubt comes a pattern of *opportunity–idea–fear–doubt–hesitation*.

3. To respond *naturally* and *spontaneously* is to be authentic and congruent.

4. As we take advantage of opportunities, circumstances develop in unexpected ways to support our choices.

## Part Four
# The Second Principle

### 22. *Principle Two*: Confidence as Our Natural State

Following the coaching session in which the first principle came to mind, I spent some time reflecting on the conversation and the positive effect it had on the client, not to mention on myself. In the course of reflecting on it, it became apparent to me that *confidence is our natural state*.

> **Key Question:**
>
> What does the idea of confidence as your natural state mean to you?

Confidence as our natural state is a very concise and simple statement, which has enormous implications for our *being confident* in the Stretch Zone (see Figure 16). What I have found is that while people immediately accept the first principle – that confidence is the absence of doubt – the second principle is met quite differently.

Confidence as Our Natural State

Figure 16

When somebody hears that confidence is our natural state for the first time, what follows is typically a moment of reflection, as that person stops and thinks perhaps for the first time about his or her own assumptions about confidence. People typically say that it sounds right intuitively, but is contrary to their experience. You might have found something similar in the exercise above.

## A Paradigm Shift

The concept of confidence as our natural state turns our understanding of confidence completely on its head. The principle challenges the paradigm that confidence is something we lack and need to learn and acquire – that knee-jerk reaction of somehow *having confidence*. Yet we usually hold this paradigm of *having confidence* with such conviction that we seldom stop to question our understanding of it.

> 'The concept of confidence as our natural state turns our understanding of confidence completely on its head.'

The second principle is a highly controversial statement with massive implications, raising a number of questions. For example, what is nature? How does it work? What effect does it have? Whose nature is it anyway? Who decides to make it my nature? How does nature develop? To what extent is nature optional? Who changes it and how does it change?

### In Summary

1. Without exception, *confidence is our natural state*, anywhere, anytime.

2. This challenges the paradigm of *having confidence* that we hold with such conviction.

3. Confidence is not something we lack and need to learn and acquire.

## 23. The Power of Mother Nature

Understanding confidence as our natural state begins with understanding nature and the power inherent in Mother Nature. Today, many of us in the West seem to think we're above nature, that we have conquered nature. Yet, while Mother Nature shatters this illusion in the form of tragic catastrophes every now and again, nature also reminds us of its power more gently in every moment, but we just don't get it.

**Key Question:**

What do we mean by nature and what effect does it have on our day-to-day experience?

### Exploring Nature

Nature refers to the *natural laws that govern human behaviour*. Dictionary.com defines nature as 'the sum total of the forces at work throughout the universe'. Nature in the form of a thunderstorm quickly reminds us of the power inherent in nature. Nature is also defined as 'the instincts or inherent tendencies directing conduct' or the 'essential properties of a thing'.

So when we speak of something's nature we are referring to that which is *inherent, innate and instinctive* and which, as a force, *directs and governs behaviour*. So we can say that it is in the nature of a cat to hunt, a fish to swim or a bird to fly. These capabilities are very much the nature of these animals and it would be difficult for them to do otherwise.

Just as we can observe the nature of an animal through its actions, so we can observe the nature of a human being through his or her actions. Nature can be described as an *energy or force that manifests in observable behaviours in the forms of thought, speech or action*. What we observe is the behaviour, which tells us something about that person's nature.

Someone who smiles a lot, seeing the lighter side of life, might be described as having a sunny nature. A focused and studious person might, in comparison, be described as having a more serious nature. While the nature itself is not directly visible to our five senses, the behaviours that arise out of it most certainly are and help us understand that person's nature.

## Nature's Nature

Of one thing we can be certain, nature is not optional. We all have a nature and we are all subject to our nature, whether we like it or not. As we are governed by our nature, a sunny person will tend to be sunny and a serious person will tend to be serious. Whether on holiday, at a party, at work or at a sports event, our nature shapes our thoughts, speech and actions.

> 'We are governed by our nature.'

What is also really interesting is the manner within which nature shapes behaviour. This is really apparent when observing animals. The way in which a bird flies or a fish swims seems absolutely *effortless*. Even with great exertion, the performance seems to be without effort and is performed with poise, beauty, efficiency and effectiveness.

> 'The way in which a bird flies or a fish swims seems absolutely effortless.'

In much the same way, when we follow our nature, our actions are effortless, efficient and beautiful. One only has to observe a loving mother caring for an upset child, to see the mother's nature manifest with effortless ease. Even under difficult circumstances, the mother will follow her nature and put the needs of the child first. That is the extraordinary power of nature and the extraordinary power and grace of a woman.

Another example is found in the posture and movements of little children. Depending on their experience, they move with effortless poise and beauty. As adults, this effortless ease and efficiency is nothing more than a distant memory and our posture and movements are characterised all too often by discomfort, tiredness, aches and pains.

Actions associated with someone's nature are said to be *natural*. When something is natural it is ordinary, normal, expected, innate, instinctive, intrinsic, spontaneous, relaxed and effortless. The American Heritage dictionary defines natural as 'characterised by spontaneity and freedom from artificiality'. Dictionary.com says that it arises 'easily or spontaneously'.

So when something is natural, it is spontaneous, instinctive and characterised by effortless ease. But what does this have to do with confidence?

## Exploring Confidence as Our Natural State

The second principle implies that it is natural for human beings to be confident anywhere, anytime. Being our nature, it would be difficult for us to feel anything other than confidence. Our confidence would be independent of external circumstances and would come from within. Our confidence would be constant, innate, effortless and without limit – a very different paradigm from that of *having confidence*.

The controversial aspect of this principle is very apparent when we consider our day-to-day experience of circumstantial confidence, which seems to be in direct opposition to the notion that confidence is our natural state.

If confidence is our natural state, we might be tempted to argue, it would not come and go. Rather than *transient*, it would be *constant*. As we have seen, when something is natural it is ordinary, normal, innate, instinctive, intrinsic, spontaneous, relaxed and effortless. Yet this is not our everyday experience of confidence.

So while the second principle and our experiences of circumstantial confidence seem to contradict each other, as soon as we broaden our understanding of nature we will discover how it all fits together.

**In Summary**

1.  Nature is an inherent, innate and instinctive force, which governs behaviour.

2.  We cannot observe nature directly, only the behaviours arising out of nature.

3.  Nature is not optional; it is a given.

4.  What is natural is done with effortless ease and efficiency.

5.  Circumstantial confidence seems to contradict confidence as our natural state.

## 24. Essential Nature vs. Acquired Nature

To resolve the apparent contradiction between the idea of confidence as our natural state and our everyday experiences of it, we need to differentiate between our essential and acquired nature. Our *essential nature* refers to our essential humanity: this is universal for all of us, regardless of our gender, culture, nationality, personality or favourite flavour of ice-cream.

Our *acquired nature* refers to our individual nature, which is superimposed over our essential nature. While our essential nature is an innate part of our humanity, our acquired nature is internalised over time throughout our formative years and later in our lives (see Figure 17).

> **Key Question:**
>
> What are the implications of differentiating between our essential nature and acquired nature?

### Internalising Nature

When the issue of our acquired and essential natures are raised in coaching, people tend to recognise them quickly and can see how they relate to one another. While it is relatively easy to understand the concept of an acquired nature, the idea of an essential nature can be a little more challenging. So what exactly is our essential nature and do we all share a common humanity? These are important questions for humanity presently and most likely at every other stage of the existence of human kind.

Essential vs. Acquired Nature

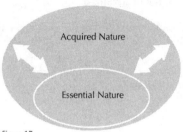

Figure 17

To understand the difference between our essential and acquired natures we only have to observe little children. When little children play, their natural spontaneity, happiness, trust, love, honesty, courage, fearlessness and innocence are usually clearly apparent. These child-like qualities are part of our essential nature.

The sound of little children playing is the same all over the world. Wherever they live, children have not had the time to internalise the normative behaviours associated with their family and culture, although this seems to be changing, with an increased pressure arising through earlier exposure to the lesser ideals of humankind. All they have to go on is their essential nature and that is why they are such spontaneous, fearless, life-loving creatures.

However, as children grow up and are exposed to other experiences, they begin to take on the ways of their family, community and culture, including the good bits and the less than good bits. Out of this socialisation process their acquired nature is born, for better or for worse.

The acquired nature superimposes itself over the child's essential nature. Sometimes the layer is light and the essential qualities continue to shine through. In other cases the acquired nature is heavy and the essential nature is less visible. It is there, but it is just covered over.

This acquired nature will naturally be different for different people. Some adults will be fun loving and playful, others serious and focused. Some will be drawn to stretching themselves and others will be content to amble along. Some are happy to follow, while some want to lead from the front.

### Happiness – Essential or Acquired

Happiness is a fundamental part of our essential nature. Everyone seeks happiness. While some may seek happiness in strange places, they seek it nonetheless. Some people, for example, seem happy when they are wallowing in their misery. Others seem to be happy when bullying others. There are those who are only happy when in a relationship; and some when they have a fast car. One way or another, we all seek happiness.

While older children, adolescents and adults all seek happiness, little children are simply happy. If you observe a baby or child closely, they are just happy. Their happiness does not come from the outside – it comes from within their *essential nature*.

As we grow older and internalise conditioned behaviours from our families, communities and cultures, we find that this inner glow of happiness seems to recede into the background and our *happiness begins to depend on objects and people* in our environment. *When I have that toy, then it will be different. When I have that new suit, then I will be happy. When I have that new car, then I will be happy*. So our happiness is no longer independent, but *object-dependent*.

When a child breaks a toy, while there may or may not be tears, the child usually just moves on and their happiness resumes effortlessly. It is as if the broken toy did not happen. With adults, when our car gets a ding or our partner says something that gets our goat, for example, our world can fall apart and we might brood on this at length. While the child has the freedom to move on, adults often become stuck and their attachments stop them from letting go and moving on.

It is important to remember, however, that the qualities associated with our essential nature do not go away as we grow up. They simply get covered over by our acquired nature. The essential nature is there; it just cannot manifest through the layers of the acquired nature.

### Confidence and Our Essential Nature

Like happiness, confidence is a fundamental part of our essential nature. It simply gets covered over, depending on our experience. The confidence is there, an essential constant within. The extent of the cover depends on the extent to which we have internalised experiences that encourage or discourage confidence.

Nasty bumps and knocks in adult life can undermine our confidence as adults. Karen, a fellow consultant, described how she was bullied by her boss and how this undermined her confidence in later life. The acquired nature does not have to continually grow, but it just might.

---

### Analogy: a Light Bulb

While doubt undermines confidence, our essential nature and inner confidence are still there waiting to shine through. If a light bulb is covered in dust and grime, the light struggles to shine through. If the bulb is clean and clear, the light shines through effortlessly. In both cases, the light is always there, a latent potential.

Richard captured a sense of this when he told me, 'Children have all the confidence in the world. They don't have any fear at all.' When we are full of doubt, the confidence cannot shine through. When the doubt disappears, the confidence is there: it did not go anywhere. Confidence is a constant, an imminent potential.

### Fearlessness – That Extraordinary Child-like State

For those who doubt that confidence is our essential nature, I think that in this instance your doubt can be a healthy thing. We all need to discover the truth for ourselves. We might be able to pick up a hint and tip here and there, but essentially we'll all have to work it out for ourselves, one way or another. And the best way is through *self-observation* and also through observing those around us – particularly in this instance the behaviour of children.

### Example: Singing in Front of a Group

Children seem to have an *absence* of that fear which adults have in *abundance*. A child will sing fearlessly in front of a group, no problem. *Will it be good enough? Will I remember the words? Will they laugh at me? Will my voice be OK? Will I get the tune right?* – these are concerns that usually will not even occur to a child. They'll simply sing to their hearts content.

When I observe my two boys at play, they are most certainly fearless. They will just launch themselves off the sofa without any doubt that Mum or Dad will catch them. As children grow older they begin to internalise apparently adult behaviours – and this is when doubt begins to set in.

> 'It took me four years to paint like Raphael, but a lifetime to paint like a child.'
>
> Picasso

Reflecting on his own experience, Andrew, a senior banker, observed, 'Just look at children: they will march into a situation and doubt has not even occurred to them.'

**In Summary**

1. To understand nature, we need to differentiate between our essential and acquired natures.

2. Our *essential nature* refers to our common humanity, which is universal to all.

3. Our *acquired nature* means the qualities and behaviours that we acquire in our life experience.

4. Like happiness, confidence is part of our essential nature and is natural for all.

## 25. Doubt as a Learnt Behaviour

If confidence is our natural state, then it must be unnatural to lack confidence and have a mindful of mindless doubt. This is why *being confident* feels so normal to us, whereas when we lack confidence it feels like something is missing – that things aren't as they should be.

---

**Key Question:**

How does doubt fit within our acquired and essential nature?

---

Confidence is part of our essential nature, a latent potential for all of us, regardless of our personalities or experience. As a basic element of our essential nature, there is no need to learn and acquire confidence – it is already there, a constant within. This means that *being confident* in the Stretch Zone is all about *creating the conditions* in which confidence can be released from within. It is simply about being ourselves.

Doubt is not our essential nature. It is a learnt behaviour that has to be acquired along the way. That is why we very rarely see little children doubting themselves or holding themselves back. Senior banker Andrew observed to me that little children 'don't have it [doubt] hard wired into them yet'.

### Learning and Internalising Doubt

Doubt is a learnt behaviour that becomes conditioned as part of our acquired nature. While doubt might be common that does not make it natural. Imaginary doubt is a transitory impostor, not a natural part of our psychological makeup (see Figure 18).

---

'While doubt might be common that does not make it natural.'

---

Although doubt is not natural to begin with, it becomes naturalised. The more that doubt becomes entrenched in our acquired nature, the more 'natural' it feels and the more difficult it is for us to behave confidently. The fact that we doubt ourselves (*that* we doubt), the things that we doubt about ourselves (*what* we doubt)

Doubt as a Learnt Behaviour

Figure 18

and the circumstances within which we doubt ourselves become conditioned habits, thereby creating a stimulus response pattern that is hardwired into our psychological system.

## Attachment and Ego-Identity

We seldom question our state of doubt for the simple reason that we are hardly, if ever, aware of it in the Stretch Zone at the *moment-of-impact*. And in those moments in which we are vaguely aware of it, we take it to be normal and 'natural', identifying with it as part of our ego-identity: the faulty mental image we hold of ourselves. In this way, we confuse what is *normal and natural* with what is *common and unnatural*.

The power underlying conditioned doubt is created by our emotional attachment to this form of doubt and our identification with it. Having few alternative perspectives available to us, we cling to this attachment with great conviction and never pause to question it. It becomes a perverse comfort zone within which we confine ourselves in order to avoid the discomfort of *stepping up* into the Stretch Zone.

Our conditioning, attachment and identification with doubt mean that we cling through ill-informed desperation to our paradigm of what we hold to be true about ourselves – and it never occurs to us that just brimming below the surface is a completely different alternative.

**In Summary**

1.  Doubt is not part of our *essential nature*. It is a learnt behaviour, part of our *acquired nature*.

2.  While doubt is not our nature, it can nevertheless feel very 'natural'.

3.  The power underling doubt is our identification and attachment to it, our ego-identity.

## 26. Nature and Circumstantial Confidence

While confidence is our natural state and part of our essential nature, as we have seen, our day-to-day experience is so often that of circumstantial confidence. This apparent contradiction makes complete sense in the context of the distinction between our acquired and essential natures.

**Key Question:**

What is the relationship between circumstantial confidence and your own acquired and essential natures?

Previously we observed that, while our confidence might seem to come and go, this is only an appearance. What is actually happening is that our learnt and acquired doubt comes and goes, covering over our natural confidence in certain circumstances. While doubt is a *transient impostor*, confidence is actually our *constant companion*.

'While doubt is a transient impostor, confidence is our constant companion.'

Confidence, as part of our essential nature, is a constant – an immediate and imminent potential. The learnt pattern of doubt within our acquired nature is transient and will cover over our confidence and essential nature only under certain circumstances within the Stretch Zone.

**In Summary**

1.  Confidence as our natural state and circumstantial confidence are not contradictory concepts.

2.  Learnt doubt within our *acquired nature* covers over our essential confidence.

3.  Doubt, as a learnt behaviour, is conditioned in relation to certain circumstances.

Part Five

# Implications and Possibilities

## 27. Implications of the Principles in Practice

So far we have explored confidence from a variety of different perspectives. Having possibly confirmed some of our original ideas about it and having challenged others, we need to understand the implications of the principles in practice. When coaching, the answers I'm given to this question often demonstrate renewed insight in my clients, creating a catalyst for real change.

**Key Question:**

What are the implications of the principles in practice in your own life?

If confidence is the *absence of doubt* and our *natural state*, there seem to be *three fundamental implications* of the principles in practice:

1. If confidence is our natural state the implication is that it is *already there*, a part of our essential nature. So the first implication is that we do not have to develop confidence at all – we only have to *create the conditions* within which it is inevitable.

2. If confidence is the absence of doubt, the implication is that in order to feel confident all we have to do is to *eliminate the doubt*. When doubt is silenced, our confidence in the Stretch Zone shines through naturally. Bound by the laws of nature, it cannot do otherwise.

3. If confidence is the absence of doubt and part of our natural state, there is not much we can *do* about it other than trust that we will be able to *deal with things as they arise*. This third implication is about *letting go and not interfering* – and allowing our performance potential to go to work.

Perhaps the most challenging of the three implications is the third. We need to let go and trust that, as part of our inner nature, our confidence will be there in the Stretch Zone when it matters most. To trust is to refrain from interfering in a very natural process.

If confidence is our natural state then – in as much as it is natural for a cat to hunt, a fish to swim or a bird to fly – it is in our nature to be confident with equal mastery. Yet in our limited paradigm and mentally hijacked state, within which we believe the worst, it appears counter-intuitive to let go and to trust ourselves and our circumstances. Distrusting ourselves, we take matters into our own hands and interfere in a very natural and powerful process. In so doing, we undermine our faculties, our confidence and performance potential.

> 'Distrusting ourselves, we take matters into our own hands and interfere in a very natural process.'

Siofra described this brilliantly to me when she said she needed to 'trust my instinct more, not have to think it through'. When we constantly have to 'think' things through we lose our natural spontaneity and miss opportunities as they arise. Procrastination is not only the thief of time; it also undermines our inner state and performance potential.

### In Summary

1. As our natural state, there is no need to develop confidence: it is already there.

2. When doubt is silenced, our confidence is bound by the laws of nature to shine through.

3. The challenge is to let go and trust ourselves – and not interfere in a very natural process.

## 28. The Mistake We Make

Desperate times call for desperate measures. When we are in an emotionally and mentally hijacked state, our desperation can make letting go and trusting ourselves seem counter-intuitive and next to impossible. Our desperate state of inadequacy compels us to start doing all that we can either to avoid the situation, *flight*, or put on a bold front, a *fight* reaction.

---

**Key Question:**

Given all that has been said previously, what mistakes might you make within a mentally and emotionally hijacked state?

---

When we are faced with a threatening situation such as presenting to the Board or having a difficult conversation, our conditioning impels us to start *doing* something to feel more confident. While different people may go about this in different ways, most of us will attempt to boost our confidence mentally, emotionally and behaviourally. While some of these efforts might be rational and helpful, much of it is just *force of habit* – a conditioned coping mechanism that is not very helpful.

*Mentally*, we 'think' through the situation and play and replay it in our minds. We might, for example, rehearse what we are going to say, how others will respond and how we'll respond in turn to that. We try to predict possible scenarios and feed our doubt in the process.

*Emotionally*, we attempt to suppress our fear and doubt by working ourselves into a state so that we are fully psyched up for the challenge.

*Behaviourally*, we may attempt to face situations by putting on a bold front, puffing out our chests, standing up straight, having direct eye contact, speaking loudly, giving a bold handshake – and wearing our lucky socks.

In these ways and many more, our desperate state creates a knee-jerk reaction and we do all that we can to boost our feelings of confidence.

## A Veneer of Pseudo-Confidence

Senior manager Helen told me that she had to make a speech at her parent's fortieth wedding anniversary. Given the importance of the occasion, the pressure was on: Helen felt that she needed to be at her best and deliver the speech of her life. She didn't want to let her parents, family and friends down – and apparently there were rather a lot of them at this special event. Helen told me how she psyched herself up, drumming up the oomph for the big moment. As we saw in Chapter 6, Helen would do the same thing at the prestigious bank where she worked, psyching herself up to face daunting situations.

As we have seen, whenever we attempt to mask our feelings of underlying inadequacy in the Stretch Zone by projecting a veneer of confidence over our suppressed fear and doubt, we end up with a facade, an outward display of pseudo-confidence that is neither convincing nor sustainable.

During his coaching with me, Andy described his experiences of this, saying, 'If you build confidence on the outside only, then you are in danger of building yourself a huge facade.' The facade is inauthentic and incongruent. Yet even when we recognise it for the falsehood that it is, this may only exacerbate our feelings of inadequacy.

When asked what confidence meant to her, Helen's insightful description included: 'being out there', 'being able to cope in situations' and 'being able to converse with anyone no matter who they are'. The central theme is that of *being oneself*, of being *yourself* – of being true to yourself. Yet our conditioned doubt compels us to do all that we can to *have confidence* or mask our true feelings in the desperate hope that we'll be able to fool people. And we seldom can.

As we have seen, when what is on the outside is out of harmony with what is on the inside, the pretence is next to impossible to sustain and the cracks quickly begin to show. However, rather than trust ourselves and let go, we interfere by suppressing fear and doubt and projecting pseudo-confidence.

In Helen's case, her anniversary speech went well. It is interesting to note that she felt that, 'The audience wanted me to do well, so I felt confident.' She went on to say of other occasions that, 'If I believe the audience does not want me to do well, I have to psyche myself up a lot more.' From her description it seems that when delivering her usual work presentations, Helen's confidence is *circumstantial*. When she feels the audience's support she is confident, but when this feeling of support is absent, her confidence diminishes.

---

**In Summary**

1. Our mentally and emotionally hijacked state makes letting go and trusting ourselves counter-intuitive.

2. Our desperation creates knee-jerk reactions whereby we do all that we can to boost our confidence.

3. What results is a strategy of *having confidence*, a veneer of pseudo-confidence.

4. Real and sustainable confidence is really about *being oneself*.

---

## 29. An Unsustainable Strategy

Happily, when we recognise the futility of swimming upstream we begin to appreciate the need to question our cherished assumptions and discover an alternative approach.

---

**Key Question:**

When you 'put on' a facade of confidence in the Stretch Zone, how does this feel and what is often the effect?

---

When analysing our own behaviours and assumptions, we may realise that a facade of pseudo-confidence is unsustainable for the following reasons:

### 1. Dependent State

A facade of pseudo-confidence is dependent on that which created it – the desperate activity that goes into drumming it up. As soon as this is stopped, the facade subsides.

### 2. Divided State

When we psyche ourselves up we are in two minds, which are at odds with one another. This inner battle makes us continually question ourselves and our capabilities.

### 3. Denial State

When we psyche ourselves up, our fear and doubt do not go away. They are only suppressed and continually push to resurface.

### 4. Draining State

Creating and sustaining the suppression of fear and projection of pseudo-confidence are really hard work. The process drains our energy at an alarming rate, leaving precious little for tackling the difficult situation itself.

### 5. Distracted State

When we psyche ourselves up our faculties or powers are distracted by the battle within ourselves. Our *outer performance* inevitably reflects the distracted state of our *inner performance*.

### 6. Dead-End State

Because a facade of pseudo-confidence is unconvincing and incongruent, the very effort that goes into boosting our confidence in this way actually undermines it even further.

### 7. Desperate State

A facade of pseudo-confidence is a desperate state. No matter how much we try to mask our desperation, it leaks out and undermines our confidence further.

### 8. Depressing State

As the spiral of fear and doubt repeats itself, we feel more and more inadequate and our self-esteem diminishes accordingly.

### 9. Defining State

When our confidence and self-esteem nosedive, we accept our mentally and emotionally hijacked state as normal and natural. And it begins to define who and what we are.

Coaching client Veronica described self-doubt as when one 'continually questions one's own beliefs and thoughts' – and she was spot on. Given all the mental gymnastics that go into this process, whereby we play and re-play the situation in our minds, we simply end up putting a lot of energy into *feeding our doubt*. Whatever we give attention to will grow – and that is what happens in this situation too: doubt grows and we find ourselves making mountains out of mole hills.

The effect is *analysis-paralysis*, whereby we find ourselves tied up in mental and emotional knots and our energy and impact is drained unnecessarily. If we become hooked up in this repetitive spiral, our capacity to break free will be substantially undermined.

---

**In Summary**

1. The facade of pseudo-confidence is a *desperate* state that *drains* energy and *distracts* from the matter in hand.

2. As we repeat the knee-jerk reaction of psyching ourselves up, our inadequacy snowballs.

---

## 30. Having Confidence vs. Being Confident

Trying to swim upstream through the repeated knee-jerk reaction of *having confidence* is, as we have seen, one option when we find ourselves in the Stretch Zone. *Being confident* is another, involving a completely different paradigm. In my experience, as soon as people hear that confidence is their natural state, the old and stale gives way to a fresh new beginning, full of potentiality.

---

**Key question:**

What does *being confident* mean to you and what makes it different from *having confidence*?

---

### The Practice of *Being Confident*

As confidence is part of our natural state, there is absolutely no need to learn and acquire it. It is already there, firmly rooted in our essential nature. If we appreciate that confidence is the absence of doubt, we can see that all we need to do to release confidence from within ourselves is to quieten the conditioned doubt in our minds. In this way, it is no longer a question of *having confidence*, but of *being confident*. We touched upon this idea briefly in Chapters 22 and 25, but let's consider it more closely now.

Confidence is not something we can *have*. We can only *be* confident in the here and now. We cannot *have* confidence now for tomorrow's difficult situation. Confidence is a state of being which is bound by the laws of nature to operate only in the present moment (see Figure 20).

---

'Confidence is not something we can have. We can only be confident in the here and now.'

---

Remember how Veronica described self-doubt as when one 'continually questions one's own beliefs and thoughts'? This simple description leads to two important questions. Whose beliefs are continually questioned? And who continually questions those beliefs? Doubt is a situation whereby the mind is divided and a person is at odds with him or herself.

Having Confidence vs. *Being* Confident

| Being Confident | = | Confidence is a State - A State of Being | → | Only be Confident in the Here & Now | → | Releasing Confidence - Human Being |

| Having Confidence | = | Confidence is not an Object/Skill - that we can 'Have' | → | Cannot 'Have' Confidence for Tomorow | → | Boosting Confidence - Human Having |

Figure 20

*Being confident* is about:

### 1. Being Oneself

To use Veronica's turn of phrase, *being oneself* implies that there are not two selves or ego-identities that are divided against each other. Someone who, for example, is full of doubt might describe the feeling as 'not being oneself' – but composed of many selves, which are at odds with each other. When one is oneself, one – i.e. you or I – is singular and rooted in one's true conscious Self, which is brimming with confidence.

### 2. Being Single-Minded

*Being single-minded* implies that we are not in two minds, one of which is continually questioning the other. However, when full of doubt we could be described as being 'in two minds' – and that inner battle undermines our confidence. When we are single-minded, our minds become razor sharp instruments and our confidence follows naturally.

### 3. Being Open-Hearted

*Open-hearted* implies that we are not juggling two emotional states, suppressing fear through a projection of pseudo-confidence. When full of doubt, however, we could be described as being 'closed hearted' and, as we suppress our fear, our passion and fire is suppressed as well. When we are open-hearted, our passion ignites our confidence.

### 4. Being Natural

*Being natural* implies that we are not juggling conflicting different natures, suppressing acquired fearful natures or projecting acquired pseudo-confident natures. When we are in the grip of doubt, our acquired nature is in direct opposition to who we really are – and we might be described as 'pretentious'. When we are our natural selves, our *essential nature* and confidence manifest themselves naturally and effortlessly.

### 5. Being Attentive

*Being attentive* implies that our attention is not distracted and divided by fears and doubts, or subject to a raging battle within. When we are caught up in doubt, our attention is constantly distracted and we could even be called 'scatter brained', as we find ourselves absentmindedly consumed by that which does not matter. When singularly attentive, we will be focused and centred within the Stretch Zone.

### 6. Being Present-Minded

*Being present-minded* implies we are not absent-mindedly re-playing what has happened in the past or imagining what might happen in the future. If full of doubt, we could find ourselves described as 'absent-minded', as we toy with our worst fears about the past and future – yet we're absent from the present. When we are present-minded our faculties are focused where it really matters.

### 7. Being Independent

*Being independent* implies our confidence is not dependent on our external circumstances. If gripped by doubt, we might be 'dependent' on the people and situations that boost our confidence. When we are independent, we become self-assured and our confidence and esteem flow naturally.

### 8. Being Congruent

*Being congruent* implies we are the same on the outside as we are on the inside. If we are consumed with doubt, we are 'incongruent' in that we attempt to mask what is going on the inside with a facade on the outside. When we are congruent, our confidence is authentic and our impact increases substantially.

### 9. Being Happy

*Being happy* implies that we are not chasing happiness through the acquisition of whatever we believe will *make* us happy. We are happy within ourselves. When we are possessed by doubt, happiness appears to be absent and we could be described as being 'miserable', which helps to divide our mindsets. When we are happy, our contentedness releases our confidence and potential.

### A Quick Fix – Our Mental and Emotional Hijacking

*Being confident* is about releasing ourselves from self-imposed attachments to misconceived perceptions within our mentally and emotionally hijacked state – and about simply trusting and *being oneself*. When asked what confidence meant to her, Siofra said it involved 'trusting my instinct more, not having to think it through'. She went on to say that it is when '[I can] go with it there and say what I want to say'. When we live under the tyranny of self-imposed doubt, we undermine all that we have the potential to be.

*Being confident* in the Stretch Zone is about stripping away the layers we acquired during our formative years and about moving from our *acquired nature* to our *essential nature*. This means we have to strip away our acquired layers of doubt and the emotional attachments and identifications that sustain them. Once stripped away, what remains is our *essential nature* – and with it comes an abundance of confidence.

---

**In Summary**

1. *Being confident* is the only sustainable alternative to *having confidence*.

2. *Being confident* is about *being oneself*, with mind and heart undivided within.

3. *Being confident* is about our attention being singularly focused.

---

4. *Being confident* is about moving from our *acquired nature* to our *essential nature*.

5. *Being confident* is about being congruent, present and happy within yourself.

6. *Being confident* is about trusting yourself and honouring your natural spontaneity.

## Part Six
# Opportunities – Here and Now

## 31. Autopilot – The Lights Are On but No One's Home

The quintessence of *being confident* is that we are conscious and present. Being confident happens at the *moment-of-impact* in a place and time called *here and now* – it never happens anywhere else. Unfortunately, the mistake that most of us make has its origins at precisely this point and all that follows reflects this fragmented beginning.

> **Key Question:**
>
> What do you understand by the term 'being on autopilot' and what effect might this state have on your performance potential?

If confidence is dependent on our being consciously present then what's the problem? When I wake up in the morning I move from being unconscious and asleep to being conscious and awake. No problem!

This is probably one of the most fundamental errors at the heart of our problems as a species. We are convinced that if we are not asleep we must be awake – and never stop to question this assumption.

The truth is that, besides waking and sleeping, there is an in-between state in which we are sort of awake but not really completely awake – only *relatively awake*. This relative state is enough to get us through the day. However, it is certainly not conducive to performing at our best.

---

**Experience: State of Autopilot**

Have you ever had the experience of driving somewhere and, having arrived, realising that you have little or no memory of the journey? What is going on there? How does it work? What effect does it have? If you cannot recall the journey, where were you at the time?

---

Experiences of this nature happen when we are on *autopilot*, when we are engaged in an activity but have little to no conscious connection with what we are doing at the time. We, at best, have a 'touch 'n go', now and then connection with what we are doing. A state of autopilot is when the lights are on but no one's home.

---

'A state of autopilot is when the lights are on but no one's home.'

---

When we are on autopilot what happens is that while we are engaged in an activity such as driving to work, for example, our mind *drifts off* elsewhere, for instance with thoughts about an argument we had with our partner that morning and what we are going to say when we get home that evening. Our thoughts drift here and there between what has happened in the past and what might happen in the future.

Every now and then we reconnect with the activity of driving, usually when something unexpected happens. However, being preoccupied with the past and future, our faculties are absent from the present as well as what is actually happening in the present. Being absent from the present, our faculties are not able to make much of an impact here and now.

### Scratching Below the Surface

When we are on autopilot what happens below the surface at a psychological level can be described as follows:

*1. Attention:* divided between our different 'thoughts' and the activity at hand, our attention becomes highly distracted and substantially undermined.

**2. *Mind:*** when our attention is divided, the mind follows suit and we end up in two minds, with one mind doing the driving, for example, and another grappling with whatever we are 'thinking' about.

**3. *Heart:*** when our minds are distracted and preoccupied with some past or future event, we become emotionally charged about an event that is not actually happening in the present.

**4. *State:*** with mind and heart thus preoccupied and distracted, our inner state becomes hijacked by inner activities that have no relevance to the present.

**5. *Senses:*** when our mind and attention are preoccupied and distracted by 'thinking', neither is connected to our five senses any longer.

**6. *Perception:*** with the mind and attention disconnected from our senses, we become disengaged and disconnected from the real world in the present moment.

**7. *Attachment:*** if our mind and heart are preoccupied with some event in the past or future, we become emotionally attached to that event and to our preferences about it.

**8. *Ego-Identity:*** as we become preoccupied and emotionally attached to that event and our desires and aversions with respect to it, our ego-identity also invests itself in the event.

**9. *Consciousness:*** when we are in an emotionally hijacked state, our attention *drifts off* and we lose our conscious connection with the present and enter into an autopilot state.

While the nine points above have been described in sequence, it is not really a process but a simultaneous state, involving all these elements.

### Another Look – Intention and Prevalence

Recognising a state of autopilot is not rocket science and in everyday speech we refer to it as *absentmindedness*, which implies that while the body is present, the mind is absent. However, while relatively easy to understand, we tend only to be aware of this state in retrospect.

What is not widely appreciated is that it is seldom, if ever, our conscious intention to drift off absentmindedly into autopilot. This happens because of conditioned habit, not conscious choice. All the 'thinking' that takes place when we are on autopilot is not a conscious, intentional, rational form of thinking, but a form of pseudo-thinking, which is unconscious, unintentional, irrational and largely irrelevant from the activity at hand (see Figure 21).

State of Autopilot

Figure 21

What is also not widely appreciated by many of us is that being on autopilot is not an occasional occurrence, but is a highly prevalent state that may actually dominate much of our day-to-day lives. Whenever I've asked people what percentage of our average day they think we spend on autopilot, the answers are consistently 60, 70, 80 or 90 per cent. Even if it is just 50 per cent, which is wishful thinking, which 50 per cent of our day is it? Because this form of pseudo-thinking is completely unintentional, how do we know that we'll *be present* in the Stretch Zone when it matters most?

---

### Analogy: Flying on Autopilot

The concept of going onto autopilot comes from an aviation context in which the pilot, a conscious individual, decides to switch the plane over to autopilot, an unconscious machine. When the pilot switches 'on to' autopilot, he or she is actually switching 'off from' the conscious practice of flying the aircraft.

---

In much the same way, when we *drift off* absentmindedly, switching 'on to' autopilot, we are actually switching 'off from' the conscious present and are never aware of it at the time.

**The Lights Are On, but No one's Home**

The trouble with being on autopilot is that, because we are mentally absent at the time, we are never aware that we are on autopilot. That is why it seems like a shock when someone drives in front of us and we are rudely awakened out of our day-dream. We never really know how much of the time we are on autopilot because we're not there at the time.

---

**Exercise: Conscious Intention**

For those doubters amongst you, pick an everyday activity such as washing the dishes, gardening or reading, and make a conscious decision to be fully conscious and attentive throughout the activity – and see what happens. Like the rest of us, you'll notice that at some point you will drift off, unintentionally thinking about things that you had no intention of thinking about.

---

So what has all this got to do with confidence? Everything! When we are on autopilot, we inadvertently create the conditions within which our fears and doubts thrive. We never intentionally decide to doubt ourselves. 'I'm really going to doubt myself now!' is just not something we do. Fear and doubt only exist so long as we are on autopilot. And because we are absentminded, we are not even aware of our doubt and the effect it is having at the time. As soon as we come out of this mentally hijacked state, we are in a position to make conscious choices and to engage with our faculties aligned within the Stretch Zone and to the challenge in hand.

---

'When we are on autopilot, we inadvertently create the conditions within which our fears and doubts thrive.'

---

*Having confidence* is when we are on autopilot, consumed by our mentally hijacked state – and we are seldom aware of what is actually happening at the time. *Being confident* is when we are conscious and present at the *moment-of-impact*. Our faculties and *essential nature* empower us with confidence from within, freeing our performance potential.

**In Summary**

1.  *Being confident* is first and foremost about being conscious and present.

2.  *Having confidence* is to exit the present by dwelling instead on fears and doubts about the past and future.

3.  Fear and doubt thrive when we are on autopilot and yet we are never aware of this at the time.

4.  The state of autopilot is characterised by an unintentional, unconscious, irrational form of pseudo-thinking.

## 32. Consciousness – An Untapped Power Within

If, above all else, consciousness is the quintessence of *being confident*, then we really need to know what we mean by consciousness and how it works.

**Key Question:**

What does consciousness mean to you and what makes it so fundamental?

*Being confident* happens only at the *moment-of-impact* in a place and time called *here and now*. So what do we mean by consciousness? Where is it? How does it work? When on autopilot, where does it go? Who am I in relation to consciousness? Is it my consciousness? Is it possible to *have* consciousness? Who is reading this book? Who is observing you read this book?

Following the last two questions, you might have noticed that you have the *ability to observe* yourself as if watching yourself from the outside. In response to the second to last question you might have noticed that you became more *aware of the activity of reading*. In response to the last question, you might have noticed that you became more *aware of yourself* reading, as if you were looking in on yourself from the outside.

As human beings we have an extraordinary capacity to be conscious of and to observe ourselves and what we are doing at the *moment-of-impact*.

### Consciousness – The Master Key

When we are present and aware of ourselves and what we are doing in the present we are in a heightened state of being. This state of 'conscious awareness' is an extraordinary state: speech and action arising within this state have extraordinary power and impact. While quite ordinary and natural on one level, what makes this state so extraordinary is the fact that we generally spend so much of our time on autopilot. To be conscious and present is uncommon and exceptional.

> 'This state of 'conscious awareness' is an extraordinary state: speech and action arising within this state have extraordinary power and impact.'

When conscious and observing the *moment-of-impact* from the viewpoint of the *conscious observer*, we are actually creating the conditions within which our confidence is released naturally. We do not need to do anything to *have confidence*. We simply need to *be confident*.

> 'To be or not to be: that is the question.' – William Shakespeare

Shakespeare captured this in his play Hamlet with the profound statement 'to be or not to be: that is the question'. This quote sums up what is being said here – that we have the choice 'to be' the conscious observer in the present or to become mentally hijacked and 'not to be'. That is the question!

In our day-to-day lives we tend 'not to be' and, as we drift off on to autopilot, our speech and actions follow the conditioning entrenched within our *acquired nature*, but we are not even aware of this at the time. This distracted, desperate and divided state means that our inner faculties become fragmented and unable to function effectively. When the conditions conducive to our *inner performance* are compromised, our confidence and *outer performance* inevitably follow suit.

**The Power of Conscious Presence**

The essence of *being confident* is that we are able to consciously observe ourselves, our state and whatever is in front of us – not in retrospect, but when it matters. Whereas it is common for people to know what they should have done with *hindsight*, it is uncommon and exceptional to be aware of your state and impact with *foresight* at the *moment-of-impact*.

We are, first and foremost, conscious beings who exist in mental, emotional and physical dimensions. The conscious observer can be defined as that overarching consciousness which observes and powers our various faculties and capabilities. With respect to this, I agree with Henry Thoreau, who said: 'I know of no more encouraging fact than the unquestioned ability of a man to elevate his life by conscious endeavour.'

> 'I know of no more encouraging fact than the unquestioned ability of a man to elevate his life by conscious endeavour.'
>
> Henry David Thoreau

When we are consciously present, the mind is connected to the senses and there is a distinct absence of that autopilot-like pseudo-thinking which misappropriates our powers and abilities. With the mind centred, all our faculties align – and confidence becomes inevitable.

We began this chapter with questions about consciousness. In truth, we cannot really *know* consciousness. We can only be aware of its presence and benefit from all that it brings. What we can say is that consciousness is not something we can *have*; we can only *be* conscious. Being conscious is about being yourself, being present, observing yourself and your environment from the viewpoint of the conscious observer.

As soon as we begin to tap into this untapped power within each of us, we start to elevate ourselves and our confidence and performance potential will flow accordingly.

**In Summary**

1. Confidence only occurs at the *moment-of-impact*, in the here and now.

2. As human beings, we have the extraordinary power of conscious *self-observation*.

3. Speech and actions that arise out of 'conscious awareness' have presence and impact.

4. Consciousness is not something we can *have*; we can only *be* conscious.

5. Being conscious, we create the conditions within which confidence is inevitable.

## 33. Self-Confidence vs. Ego-Confidence

Confidence is often referred to as *self-confidence*. I find it intriguing that we do not refer to it as *ego-confidence*, yet that is what we spend most of our time trying to *have* and acquire.

> **Key Question:**
>
> How would you differentiate between self-confidence and ego-confidence?

### *Having Confidence vs. Being Confident*

As a strategy, *having confidence* is nothing other than *ego-confidence*. When your mentally hijacked state is on autopilot, your entrenched and conditioned ego will attempt to acquire the confidence it believes it lacks by psyching itself up through all sorts of trickery.

Our ego refers to the mental image we hold of ourselves, our self-image. It is not who we are, but a mental construct that we acquire and *have* over time. The ego is an idea, an impostor, a pretender, a figment of our imagination. And it is unconscious and always untrue (see Figure 22).

Self-Confidence vs. Ego-Confidence

Figure 22

As an identity, the ego associates 'I' with some conditioned notion about ourselves; for example: 'I am not confident', 'I am not good enough', 'I am good looking', 'I am the best' and so on. Positive or negative, an ego-identity is a self-imposed limitation as it excludes more than it includes.

In fact, ego-confidence is built upon the shaky foundations of something that only exists within our imagination – in this case, our ego. A mental construct or imagining that is built on top of another mental construct or imagining is guaranteed to fade very quickly, and it does.

The strategy of *being confident* is entirely different to that of *having confidence*. When confidence comes from within, the source of our confidence is our inner being, our conscious self and *essential nature*. Coming naturally from within, it is abundant, congruent, real and sustainable.

While *having confidence* is about ego-confidence, *being confident* is about self-confidence and, as we have seen, the experience and impact are completely different.

---

**In Summary**

1.  *Ego-confidence* is a facade of pseudo-confidence, an impostor and pretence.

2.  *Self-confidence* is our natural state, which comes from within.

---

## 34. Inner Idiot vs. Inner Sage

If genuine self-confidence is about *being confident* rather than *having* ego-confidence, what compels us to waste so much effort and energy in psyching ourselves up to create a facade of pseudo-confidence in the first place?

---

**Key Question:**

What drives you, for example, to repeatedly pursue ego-confidence rather than genuine self-confidence?

---

The wise say that to become what we are, we need to come out of what we are not. To become what we are, we need to come out of the limiting paradigms, convictions and attachments that we hold with such conviction and see them for the impostors they are. As soon as we come out of our limiting paradigms new opportunities begin to emerge.

---

'The wise say that to become what we are, we need to come out of what we are not.'

---

### The Inner Idiot

We are driven to cling to the wishful thinking that ego-confidence is going to work for us by our *inner idiot*. The inner idiot is the ego-identity that thrives, along with the fear and doubt, whenever we are on autopilot. The ego-idea that 'I am not a confident person' is taken as a fundamental truth about who and what we are – and this conviction compels us to *have* what we believe we lack.

Within the limited world of the ego-identity, the idea that 'I lack confidence' becomes completely true. Under this false assumption, it is only logical to acquire or 'have' what we lack, as in *having confidence*. And, as our outer performance reflects our inner turmoil, the ego finds the means it needs to justify its identification with the idea that 'I am not a confident person'.

The inner idiot or ego can never see beyond the limited confines of its comfort zone. While the inner idiot thinks it knows best, it is, in fact, completely ignorant of all that lies outside its limited world. It is ignorant because it ignores all the possibilities that are outside its conditioning and, as it fights for its very survival, it does all that it can to maintain this ignorance.

The inner idiot is a complete dunce, a moron, a fool and any other derogatory description you can possibly think of. It always has been and always will be. You can never really educate the inner idiot as its very survival depends on its ignorance.

## Our Inner Sage

Whenever we come out of autopilot and reconnect with the conscious observer in the here and now, the inner idiot skulks away into the shadowy world from whence it came. In the absence of the superimposition of the inner idiot what emerges out of this completely different state is our conscious self – the sage within.

The conscious observer is the *inner sage*, reflecting our innermost wisdom as a fundamental part of our essential nature. While the inner idiot is a complete dunce, the inner sage is full of wisdom, temperance and intention.

*1. Wisdom:* in the absence of the mental hijacking that thrives on autopilot, our inner sage offers us the wisdom with which to see things as they are and to speak and act with insight and integrity.

*2. Temperance:* in the absence of emotional hijacking, our inner sage reflects an emotional maturity and self-regulation that channels our energy with strength and humility.

*3. Intention:* in the absence of a mentally or emotionally hijacked state, our inner sage holds all our faculties in tension, aligned and focused, and follows through in speech and action with resolute intention.

When we access the wisdom, temperance and intention of our inner sage, we will find that we are capable beyond all our preconceived expectations, even in the Stretch Zone. These qualities are part of our *essential nature*, just waiting to be discovered and nurtured with practice. With wisdom, temperance and intention, *being confident* is simply not an issue. The real issue is how we use our confidence.

To become what we are, we need to come out of what we are not. The bottom line is that we have a choice. We can either follow the *inner idiot* or we can follow the *inner sage*. In the movie *Star Wars*, Obi-Wan Kenobi asks: 'Who is the greater fool, the fool or the fool who follows the fool.' What a great question!

---

'Who is the greater fool, the fool or the fool who follows the fool?'

Obi-Wan Kenobi

---

Can you imagine for a moment if, as a species, we were all able to access our inner sage and act with wisdom, temperance and intention? Our world would be completely transformed from the chaotic disruptions that so characterise our outcast state. Our crimes as a species arise out of fear. To be free from fear and doubt is to discriminate the inner sage from the inner idiot, whose very existence is our most essential crime, which we all impose on ourselves and each other.

---

**In Summary**

1. To become what we are, we need to come out of what we are not.

2. The ego is the inner idiot, which thinks it knows best but cannot see beyond its limited world.

3. The conscious observer is our inner sage, full of wisdom, temperance and intention.

4. 'Who is the greater fool, the fool or the fool who follows the fool?'

---

## 35. The Master Key – Conscious Observer

The master key to *being confident* and coming out of the dominion of the inner idiot is consciousness itself. Without consciousness nothing would happen and with consciousness everything becomes a possibility.

> **Key Question:**
>
> What is the difference between consciousness and 'thinking'?

As mentioned previously, defining consciousness is next to impossible. However, what we can do is recognise consciousness by its presence, quality and effect.

### Consciousness and Thinking

While defining consciousness, like confidence, is very difficult, it is possible to identify what it is not. Whenever consciousness comes up in coaching or training, I'll ask, 'What does consciousness mean to you?' The response almost always associates consciousness with thinking, with the underlying idea being that when we are thinking we are conscious. Mistake!

René Descartes' famous quote 'I think, therefore I am' sums up this perspective perfectly, associating existence and consciousness – 'I am' with thinking. And yet nothing could be further from the truth. The effect on our day-to-day lives of this perspective is relentless (see Figure 23).

Consciousness & Thinking

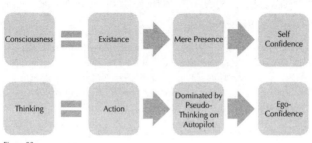

Figure 23

Firstly, thinking is an activity that takes place in the mind. Consciousness is the existence or presence that observes that thinking. However, to be conscious in no way requires thinking. We can easily recognise the truth of this whenever we are shocked in some way or find ourselves in awe of a beautiful sunrise. Within these sorts of state, stillness arises as we become conscious – and there is a distinct absence of thinking.

Secondly, most of our thinking, the pseudo-thinking that thrives when we are on autopilot, is unintentional and unconscious. So to associate thinking with consciousness is madness. Within the limited world of the ego-identity, thinking is the consciousness of the inner idiot. When the thinking stops, its existence stops. However, given the nature of this paradigm it is not surprising that we associate thinking with consciousness.

---

**Exercise: Conscious Awareness**

This is something you can observe for yourself. Take a moment and, wherever you are, just be conscious and present at the *moment-of-impact*. Practising *self-observation*, observe what happens in relation to thinking, consciousness and stillness. Make every effort to be completely still and fully conscious, not thinking of anything.

---

Another way to differentiate between consciousness and thinking is to recognise that whereas consciousness is complete stillness, thinking is movement. They are mutually exclusive. This does not mean that we cannot think consciously. It just means that most of our thinking – that autopilot-like, pseudo-thinking – is not conscious. This is the master key!

### Recognising the Inner Sage

If our consciousness and inner sage form the master key between them, how can we recognise them and follow their wisdom? Of one thing we can be sure: the inner sage will not be standing on the roof tops, as it were, shouting its head off to get our attention. That is what the inner idiot does.

Have you ever noticed that in life it is usually the biggest ego that that makes the most noise, talking incessantly about him- or herself? In contrast, people with integrity and presence tend to speak in measured tones, without any need to show off.

Similarly, you can be sure that the voice within you that is incessantly mouthing off is the voice of your inner idiot. Whether it is putting you down or boosting you up, the voice of the inner idiot is an incessant, loud, distracting, emotional noise that just does not know when enough is enough. Verbal diarrhoea!

In contrast, the inner sage can be recognised by the quality of its voice within, which is quieter, measured, rational, detached and compassionate. Given all the noise of the inner idiot, the voice of the inner sage is easily missed.

So whenever you observe that incessant noise within, know it to be the inner idiot trying to impose its way. And whenever you hear that composed, quiet and rational voice within, that is your inner sage, the voice of reason.

The saying goes: 'to master one thing is to master all; to try to master all is to master nothing'. The one thing that needs to be mastered is the ability to listen to yourself, your inner sage.

> 'To master one thing is to master all; to try to master all is to master nothing.'
>
> Anon

**In Summary**

1. Consciousness is the master key to *being confident*.

2. Consciousness and thinking are two different things.

3. Thinking is an activity in the mind. Consciousness is that which observes the thinking.

4. While the inner idiot mouths off incessantly, the inner sage is measured, calm and composed.

## 36. Unlearning the Doubt

If we define confidence as the *absence of doubt* and *our natural state*, we can see that *being confident* is not so much about our learning something new as it is about *un-learning the doubt*.

> **Key Question:**
>
> What actually is doubt and what might it mean to *un-learn* it?

Unlearning doubt requires that we understand it first. Previously we said *what* we doubt is not as important as *that* we doubt it. We also said that knowledge of our doubt is insufficient. Awareness of doubt in the present is the key factor. So what actually is doubt?

Underlying the diverse responses that I've heard to this question over the years is a consistent theme. Alison told me that doubt is 'when you start questioning yourself, your approach, your understanding, everything'. Karen said that, for her, doubt often involves 'telling myself that I can't'. She went on to give an example of a skiing trip during which she kept telling herself, 'I'm going to fall over' – and she duly did. Veronica described doubt as 'continually questioning your own beliefs or thoughts', which creates an 'inability to think clearly'. Siofra described doubt as 'constantly questioning, is this the right thing to do'.

The central theme of these definitions is that doubt is nothing other than *thinking in the mind*. Yet no one over the years has ever described it to me as succinctly as that. Doubt is not rational, conscious, deliberate thinking, but irrational, habitual, unintentional, autopilot-like pseudo-thinking in the mind.

It is almost as though doubt is a voice within us – the *voice of doubt*, with a life of its own, sitting on our metaphorical shoulders and undermining our confidence and performance potential whenever we are in the Stretch Zone. Doubt is usually *telling us that we can't* or *questioning our ability that we can*.

> 'Doubt is usually telling us that we can't or questioning our ability that we can.'

## Voice of Doubt

The voice of doubt is the mouthpiece of the inner idiot. When we are in the power of the inner idiot, the inner voice of doubt is experienced as a reality in much the same way that a dream seems like a reality at the time of dreaming. When we wake up, however, we quickly become aware that it was only a dream and we forget about it and move on.

Similarly, the moment we become aware of doubt, the power of that inner critic diminishes – as does its impact. Like a dream, doubt is a fiction that has no existence within the real world. It only exists within our private world: no one else even knows it exists unless we tell them about it. While not part of the real world, its presence and impact are relentless nonetheless.

Andy described doubt to me as 'a state of disbelief, not a state of reality' and went on to say that it is a 'self-imposed belief state' which we create ourselves. Richard said, 'Doubt is questioning your ability to do something. It's man-made; that is, we create it ourselves'. Andrew summed it up, saying: 'It is a mental barrier that you create for yourself.'

## A Full Deck

The voice of doubt is not something to worry about in the sense of hearing voices or losing your mind. We all have these voices or thoughts banging about in our minds. This doesn't mean we are a couple of cards short of a deck.

While, as we have seen, irrational 'thinking' is a universal phenomenon, we are usually simply not aware of it. Martin described this, saying, 'Cogs are always turning in my head,' and disclosing, 'I lose confidence when I'm speaking to myself in my own head, when I'm being self-critical.' Richard also spoke of this process, saying, 'It's that autopilot thing. I slip back into my old ways'.

So how do we deal with the *voice of doubt* in the mind?

## Un-creating the Doubt

Of one thing we can be certain, doubt is created by no one other than ourselves. You can be sure that no one else even knows you doubt yourself. So, as the creator of our doubt, all we need to do is to stop creating it.

> 'As the creator of our doubt, all we need to do is to stop creating it.'

Within the private world in which our doubt thrives, we are, in a manner of speaking, the lord and creator of all. As the sovereign lord, all we have to do is to become aware of the doubt and *un-create it*. Instead of feeding doubt with our attention, we un-create it by focusing our attention elsewhere – onto something more constructive.

### In Summary

1. Doubt is nothing other than irrational, unintentional, autopilot-like pseudo-thinking.

2. Doubt usually tells us that we can't or questions our ability that we can.

3. The voice of doubt is the mouth piece of the inner idiot.

4. No one else is aware of our doubt. It is entirely our own creation.

5. As doubt is our own creation, getting rid of the doubt is about our *un-creating* it.

6. *Un-creating doubt* is about cutting off its power by focusing our attention elsewhere.

## 37. The Moment-of-Impact

*Being confident* only happens in a place and time called here and now, at the *moment-of-impact*. Yet, despite the fact that confidence can only occur in the present moment, we waste considerable effort and energy trying to project ego-confidence into the future.

---

**Key Question:**

What is it about the *moment-of-impact* that makes it potentially so transformational?

---

The present moment is the only moment we can influence. The past has passed and the future is yet to come. Neither the past nor the future can be directly influenced by mortal man. What we can do is positively influence the present: the *moment-of-impact*.

---

'The present moment is the only moment we can influence.'

---

One might argue that by influencing the present we can shape the future. That, however, merely confirms that the only *moment-of-impact* is the present moment. The good news is that it is always the present moment – it is *never not now*. So what does this have to do with confidence?

### Impact Now!

If confidence is the absence of doubt, un-creating our doubt needs to happen in the present, at the *moment-of-impact*. Knowing what we doubt about ourselves is not that relevant. That knowledge is of the past, an *ordinary knowledge* that is old and stale. Unless we are aware of our doubt at the *moment-of-impact*, that ordinary knowledge is not much use.

The key to unlearning doubt is to be aware of it at the *moment-of-impact*. While knowledge is necessary, it is not sufficient: we must also be aware of it in that moment. The knowledge that arises at the *moment-of-impact* is a *special knowledge* which illuminates what needs to be known at that particular moment in time.

> ## Example: a Golf Swing
>
> A prior knowledge, or theory, of how to hold and swing a golf club will not make for an excellent shot if a golfer ignores what is taking place at the moment she takes her swing. The golfer might notice that there are obstacles on the fairway, that her glove is slippery, that there is a stiff breeze or that she is upset about her previous shot. How much power, deflection and cut to put into the swing can only be known at the *moment-of-impact*.
>
> These factors represent the *special knowledge* that arises in the present moment and can make all the difference between a mediocre shot and a world-class shot.

This is not to dismiss knowledge that we have accumulated in the past, which is naturally important. It would not be very helpful if we continually had to learn how to walk, for example. It is, however, limited in that it is not necessarily specific to what is taking place in the present.

While it is always now – the nature of time means that we are continually at the *moment-of-impact* – the content of that 'now' is constantly changing as events unfold. Because the content is ever evolving, we need to make sure that we remain present within the evolving moment so that we can deal with things effectively.

### That Untapped Power Within

What makes the *moment-of-impact* so powerful is that it is the only means whereby we can access the conscious present and our inner sage. As soon as we come into the present, our consciousness and inner sage come into effect with all their potentiality.

When we are in the moment, there is an absence of doubt. Fear and doubt thrive when we are absentmindedly consumed by the past and the future. The *moment-of-impact* is about the present and within the present there is an absence of doubt.

The *moment-of-impact* empowers by virtue of what it enables – the promptings of our inner sage – and by what it disables – our fear and doubt and *inner idiot*. When empowered in this way, there is nothing that we cannot face.

**In Summary**

1. *Being confident* can only happen in the here and now, at the *moment-of-impact*.

2. *Having confidence* is about projecting confidence into an imaginary future.

3. Our full power and consciousness comes into effect at the *moment-of-impact*.

## 38. Conscious Choice or Conditioned Choice

Silencing the inner idiot is simple, but not necessarily easy to do. We may often find that our best intentions remain not much more than that – intentions – and we end up repeating familiar patterns of frustratingly unproductive behaviour.

---

**Key Question:**

What drives you to constantly repeat frustratingly unproductive behaviours in your own life?

---

A standard paradigm of human performance is based on the assumption that we can access conscious choice as a matter of course. We believe that we navigate our lives through our choices and intentions on a daily basis. This is, unfortunately, not necessarily the case. When it matters most, our best intentions frequently do not translate into realities.

Similar to the common assumption that when we wake up in the morning we are fully awake and conscious throughout the day, the idea that we have conscious choice is no more than wishful thinking. While we most certainly have the potential for conscious choice, within our day-to-day state our capacity for conscious choice is substantially limited.

### Autopilot and Conditioned Choice

When we switch *off from* the present, *on to* autopilot, our mentally hijacked state dramatically undermines our capacity for conscious choice. Experience demonstrates that when we are on autopilot we are hardly aware of the choices available to us in the first place and we blunder on repeating the same old, same old mistakes.

---

'When we switch off from the present, on to autopilot, our mentally hijacked state dramatically undermines our capacity for conscious choice.'

---

As we repeat our conditioned habits we strengthen the inner idiot's dominance and further entrench ourselves in our conditioned behaviour. And we are usually none too aware of what we are doing to ourselves at the time. Because we believe we *are* our ego-identities, we never think to question this sorry state – and the negative spiral continues day-in and day-out.

## Conscious Choice and the *Moment-of-Impact*

Conscious choice is completely dependent on the extent to which we are conscious and present at the *moment-of-impact*. While our choices within a state of autopilot are completely conditioned, our choices when we are present are conscious and intelligent.

> 'Conscious choice is completely dependent on the extent to which we are conscious and present at the moment-of-impact.'

As soon as we come out of our mentally hijacked state into the present, conscious choice becomes a distinct possibility. When we are present we reconnect with the moment-of-impact and the conscious observer or inner sage resumes its rightful place as our inner guide. With the inner sage at the helm, we begin to see the wood for the trees and, seeing things as they are, we start to make informed and appropriate choices to the best of our ability (see Figure 24).

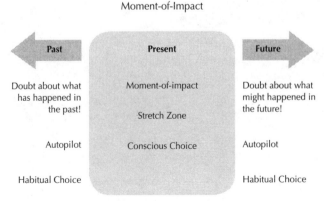

Figure 24

As I suggested at the start of this chapter, silencing the *inner idiot* is simple, but not necessarily easy to do. The momentum that drives it is substantial. Even when the inner idiot has been silenced once, it is likely to raise its head again and again. The key to shutting up the inner idiot is to silence consistently the voice of doubt whenever it raises its unwanted head. We'll be looking at practical ways to do this in Part Seven. With consistent practice, the tables will turn and the inner idiot will lose its dominance in our lives.

### In Summary

1. Within our current paradigm, our choices are so often limited to *conditioned choice*.

2. When on autopilot under the inner idiot, conscious choice is not that likely.

3. *Conscious choice* becomes a possibility when we come out of autopilot into the present.

## Part Seven
# Practices and Techniques

## 39. Techniques for Releasing Confidence

Without day-to-day practical application, all the knowledge in the world would be of very little value – no more than mere mental gymnastics. Applying the insights in these pages in practice is to discover the secret to *being confident* in the Stretch Zone, when it really matters.

---

**Key Question:**

When you've been in your Stretch Zone in the past, what techniques have you used to feel more confident?

---

### Creating the Conditions for *Being Confident*

The techniques that I have presented in this book are not designed to *develop, build or boost* confidence. They are designed to create the conditions within which confidence is inevitable. While boosting pseudo-confidence only channels our energy into feeding our doubt, these practical techniques will create the conditions whereby confidence is released from within.

---

'The techniques that I have presented in this book are not designed to develop, build or boost confidence. They are designed to create the conditions within which confidence is inevitable.'

---

The conditions that are most propitious for genuine confidence arise when we come out of autopilot and the mentally and emotionally hijacked state of the inner idiot with its *defined possibilities*, and enter the realm of the conscious observer with its *undefined possibilities*.

Referring to the exercise above, to what extent do the techniques you've practised in the past relate to a strategy of developing and *having confidence* – or releasing your inner confidence and *being confident*?

**Primary and Secondary Techniques**

In Chapter 2, we differentiated between an *inside out* and an *outside in* approach to releasing confidence. As will be clear by now, in this book I want to emphasise the value of releasing confidence from the *inside out*. This can be achieved through a range of primary techniques that create the conditions within which confidence manifests naturally. I will, however, also be highlighting some secondary techniques that can enhance confidence from the *outside in*, particularly when used in support of the primary techniques.

The primary techniques are all based on one foundation technique – the practice of conscious awareness, as described in the next chapter. All the other primary techniques are variations on this central theme of transforming our inner state through the power of our conscious awareness. By varying the application of this foundation technique, we will provide ourselves with a repertoire of techniques that are applicable to different sets of circumstances. In essence, however, they are very much one and the same thing.

The secondary techniques that I will be discussing include: goal setting, self-coaching, feedback, relationship building, and practices relating to knowledge, humour and perspective. We'll also explore confidence-like behaviours and the inner and outer feedback loops.

---

**In Summary**

1. The techniques are not designed to *develop* confidence or support the faulty strategy of *having confidence*.

2. The techniques are designed to create the conditions for releasing our inner confidence and *being confident*.

3. Supporting the *inside out* approach are secondary techniques for working from the *outside in*.

---

## 40. The Practice of Conscious Awareness

Releasing confidence from within begins with a conscious choice. Without the capacity for conscious choice, it is next to impossible for us to come out of autopilot and enter into the realm of the inner sage. Consciousness remains the master key.

> **Key Question:**
>
> Given what you have heard so far, how would you describe the practice of conscious awareness?

*The practice of conscious awareness* means connecting the mind and senses through the faculty of attention (see Figure 25). When the mind and senses of touch, sight, taste, smell and hearing are connected, the mind naturally quietens down and can even come to a point of stillness – a *heightened state of readiness* for action. As the mind quietens, our emotions follow suit and we feel a calm poise and composure.

> 'The practice of conscious attention means connecting the mind and senses through the faculty of attention.'

When we bring the mind and heart to stillness, we are, in effect, proactively changing our state, exiting the autopilot-like state of relative consciousness and entering a more awake state of increased consciousness. The consciousness itself has not changed in any way; it was always there. What has changed is our connection with it.

Practice in Conscious Awareness

Figure 25

When quietening the mind and heart, we tune out of our imaginary, private world of pseudo-thinking and tune in to the real world to which we need to respond. We become more self- and situation-aware, very much in touch with ourselves and with what is around us.

---

**The Practice of Conscious Awareness**

Sit in a relaxed and upright posture with your feet on the floor and hands on your lap. Your eyes can be open or closed, more or less directed down towards the floor in front of you. Then, having read them through first, follow the steps below.

1. ***Touch:*** sitting relaxed and comfortable, become aware of the sense of touch. Be aware of your physical body. Be aware of any tensions in your body, in your eyes, face, jaw, neck, shoulders, back and legs. Allow these unnecessary tensions to release and relax. Be aware of your feet on the floor, the weight of your body on the seat and back of the chair, the play of cool air on your face and hands. Being aware of your physical body through your sense of touch, simply hold that awareness.

2. ***Sight:*** turn your attention to your sense of sight and, opening your eyes if they were closed, become fully aware of whatever is in front of you. There is no need to look around; simply be aware of what is immediately in front of you. Notice the colours, shapes, textures and forms. You might notice that your mind wanders off, unintentionally, thinking about and commenting on this or that. As soon as you notice this, bring your attention back to your sense of sight. Hold that awareness.

3. ***Taste:*** be aware of the sense of taste in your mouth. You might have just brushed your teeth or had some coffee – and that taste is lingering on. Whatever it is, simply allow your attention to rest and focus on the sense of taste, practising disinterest in any other distractions that the ego-identity might present via the 'thinking' mind. Be fully aware of the sense of taste and rest in that awareness.

---

4. **Smell:** turn your attention to your sense of smell and be aware of whatever this sense perceives. There might be an aroma of perfume in the air or the smell of food about. Again, regardless of what it is that you smell, simply rest your attention on the sense of smell. You might notice that your attention wanders on a tangent, 'thinking' about something or the other. If you notice this happen, simply return your attention to the sense of smell and rest in that awareness.

5. **Hearing:** finally, tune in to your sense of hearing and become fully aware of the sounds around you. You might find that your mind picks up a particular sound and wanders off on some unintended tangent. As soon as this occurs, simply return your attention to the sense of hearing and listen fully to the sounds that are around the room. Allow your hearing to range far and wide, to the distant sounds out and about as well as those close by. You might notice you become more aware of sounds like a clock ticking or the air con, sounds of which you were previously unaware. Simply attend to these sounds and rest in that awareness.

Having completed these steps, open your eyes again, if necessary, and observe your increased stillness and consciousness. Notice what happens next.

*The practice of conscious awareness* is most certainly not my creation, but is a technique that has been around for a very long time. Having practised the exercise for some fifteen years, I have found it to be invaluable in all aspects of life, including family, work, relationships, sport and recreation. It is, in essence, a form of meditation that has been around since time began, but which has been largely forgotten in our hurry-up world. Exercises of this nature are, however, becoming far more commonplace today. Nowadays there is not only greater openness about them but an increased appetite for these sorts of practices.

Having initially told me, 'I come across as confident, but I am not,' Jenny, a manager, commented that practising conscious awareness was like 'slipping in and out of thinking and not thinking'. Siofra, when trying out the practice for the first time, described it as the mind 'slowing down' and noted, 'It is incredibly relaxing – you just don't let your mind label things.' Having performed the exercise a few times, Siofra went on to say, 'It clears your mind of all that stuff that creeps in.' She continued, 'I find it so refreshing that I can clear my mind,' adding that, 'When focusing on your senses it [the mind] quietens down.'

When reflecting on her experience, Siofra summarised her sentiments: 'It is that inner state that is why I feel so much more in control, calm, relaxed'. The experience is one of increased conscious awareness and choice as to our thoughts, speech and actions.

The exercise cannot be known in theory, so if you have not tried it already, I would strongly suggest that you do so right now. Don't fuss about getting it right – just enjoy the general sense of it with a light touch and sense of play.

> 'He tastes nothing who has not tasted for himself.'
>
> Marcilio Ficino

As we have seen, conscious awareness is the master key and it can only really be understood in practice. No amount of thinking or academic enquiry will enable you to truly understand your capacity for consciousness awareness. As soon as you change your state and come fully into the present, you will find that there is increased space between action and reaction, which will enable you to come out of the shadow of the conditioned behaviours of your *acquired nature* and make some conscious choices here and now.

**In Summary**

1. *The practice of conscious awareness* means connecting mind and senses through your attention.

2. When the mind and senses are connected, *pseudo thinking* in the mind quietens down.

3. As the mind quietens down, fears and anxieties follow suit accordingly.

4. By quietening your mind and heart, you can change your state and readiness for conscious action.

## 41. The Practice – Observations and Effect

With diligent practice, the effects and benefits of the exercise described in Chapter 40 will become clearly apparent. Because consciousness is the master key, the benefits of practising conscious awareness are limitless and, as I have suggested, are applicable to any situation, including home, relationships, work, sport, acting and many other activities.

---

**Key Question:**

What did you observe when practising conscious awareness and what effect did the practice have?

---

One of the primary observations with the practice is that, while the aim is to still incessant pseudo-thinking in the mind, the mind very quickly finds its way back on to autopilot and into pseudo-thinking. So how does this work?

### Labelling and Commenting

Practising conscious awareness, we may discover that our normally restless minds are conditioned to *label* things. As soon as an impression is perceived through the senses in the exercise, the mind may rush to label that impression. What follows is a stream of unintentional pseudo-thinking or commentary about the impression. And before we know it we're back on autopilot, under the dominion of the inner idiot.

---

**Example: Labelling People, Objects and Situations**

If, while practising conscious awareness, we were to hear someone speak, our inner idiot would very likely rush to identify the individual – labelling them as Kevin, for example. What follows is a stream of pseudo-thinking about what we think and feel about Kevin, all based on past attachments and future projections.

At no point did we make a *conscious choice* to think these thoughts; it is an entirely *conditioned choice*. And before we know it our mental state is hijacked and we are disconnected from the conscious present, the *moment-of-impact*.

---

In her observation about the practice, Siofra observed that it meant 'you just don't let your mind label things'. As soon as we start labelling we start thinking – typically that mindless, conditioned, pseudo-thinking within which the inner idiot thrives.

When practising conscious awareness, as soon as you observe that you've gone off on a tangent through pursuing an unintentional 'thought' process, all you need to do is to return the mind to the present by re-connecting it to your senses through the power of attention. As soon as that connection is made the pseudo-thinking disappears.

---

**A Word of Caution**

Reading about the effects and benefits of the practice often results in people looking for the benefits whilst practising. However, as soon as we start to look for the results we are not really practising but 'thinking' about the result we want. This is exactly what we're trying to address.

---

Bearing this in mind, you might like to practise the exercise for a few days or weeks before reading the section below. Feel free if necessary to skip to the next chapter, which looks at how the practice actually works. Once you feel you have explored the exercise adequately for yourself, come back to this section.

The main thing when practising conscious awareness is to focus on the actual practice itself and not the results. If the practice is true, the results will be inevitable: they cannot be otherwise.

---

**Effects and Benefits**

When we connect our mind with our senses through the faculty of attention we are, in effect, creating the conditions within which a number of effects or benefits become inevitable.

1.  **Mind:** we become aware of our mental state and of 'thinking'. As pseudo-thinking quietens down, the mind sharpens into a creative and powerful instrument.

2. **Heart:** we become aware of our emotional state, with its highs and lows. As our emotional instability calms, we discover renewed energy, resilience and enthusiasm.

3. **Awareness:** with the quieting of mind and heart, we enjoy a heightened state of conscious awareness. We are more in touch with ourselves and those around us.

4. **Perception:** with awareness, our senses and perception become more acute and we switch on to the world around us with increased powers of observation.

5. **Detached Interest:** as negative emotions subside, we become more objective, not hooked in and swayed by passing preferences.

6. **Choice:** as habitual conditioning gives way to increased awareness, we move from *conditioned choice* to an increased capacity for *conscious choice*.

7. **Identity:** we begin to dissociate ourselves from our limited *ego-identity*, the inner idiot, and align ourselves with the conscious observer, our inner sage.

8. **Attention:** as the mind quietens we have an increased capacity for focused attention in the sustainable manner of a master craftsman, artist, athlete or sage.

9. **Energy:** with increased conscious awareness, we find we have access to a greater source of energy, which becomes more abundant and readily available.

10. **Nature:** as our *acquired nature* and conditioned habits recede, our *essential nature* comes through and we discover new qualities surfacing from within ourselves.

11. **Behaviour:** rather than react out of conditioned habit, we enjoy an increased space and conscious choice between *stimulus and response*, action and reaction.

12. **Time:** our experience of time changes. While sixty seconds remains sixty seconds, our experience and perception of time slows down, allowing the space for poised action.

*13.* **Presence:** as the mind and heart quieten we become more present at the *moment-of-impact* and our presence and gravitas expand quite naturally.

*14.* **Confidence:** in the absence of doubt, confidence releases naturally from within, enabling us to be at our best in the Stretch Zone when it matters most.

While the effects outlined above are not exhaustive, they do give a general picture of some of the more universal outcomes of the practice of conscious awareness. The important thing is to keep our attention on the practice itself, not on what we would like to get out of the practice. With diligent practice, the effects and benefits will follow quite naturally.

---

### In Summary

1.  When genuinely practising conscious awareness, the benefits and effects will follow, inevitably.

2.  Looking for the results is ego-orientated and undermines the practice itself.

3.  Practising conscious awareness changes our inner state, bringing the mind and heart to presence and stillness.

4.  The hijacked mind will attempt to label things, diverting you onto a 'thinking' tangent – on to autopilot.

---

## 42. Inner Psychology of Confidence

The practice of conscious awareness is a timeless and transformative exercise that, when followed diligently, can bring about a complete paradigm shift in how we view ourselves and our performance potential. While transformative, it is so very simple and readily available to anyone from any walk of life. So how does it work?

> **Key Question:**
>
> From your observations, what would you say is the secret behind the practice?

Practising conscious awareness is almost childlike in its simplicity and cuts through all the psycho-babble by going to the heart of the matter. However, while simple, it is not necessarily easy – as you may have discovered already. To understand the secret behind the practice we need to understand the nature of the mind and senses, and the power behind our faculty of attention.

### The Nature of the Mind

Essentially, the nature of the mind is to move, to be active – and the mind is active through thinking. The mind seems to be 'thinking' practically all the time, in a seemingly never-ending stream of thoughts. Even in sleep, the mind is active when we are dreaming. It is a restless creature, yet with incredible potential.

> 'The nature of the mind is to move, to be active – and the mind is active through thinking.'

When on autopilot, the mind habitually becomes caught up in an unending cycle of unintentional pseudo-thinking. There is a wonderful traditional story that I heard many years ago which puts across the nature of the mind beautifully – and it goes like this…

## The Householder and the Monkey, a Traditional Story

There was once a householder who was not happy with the fact that he always had so much work to do around the house, besides at his job in order to earn a living. So he went to a wise man for advice on how to turn this unfortunate situation around. Hearing the householder's story, the wise man said he had a solution to the problem: the householder should go home and help would arrive the next day. So the householder dutifully went home and the next day there was a knock on the door. When he opened the door, the householder found a monkey waiting to enter. The monkey said that he had been sent to help, but there was a condition. (Even in traditional stories there is no such thing as a free lunch!) The condition was that the householder had to keep the monkey constantly busy.

The householder thought this was wonderful and got the monkey going with his first task. Off the monkey went to wash the dishes. Within minutes the animal was back, looking for the next job. The householder thought this was the best thing and told the monkey to clean the kitchen from top to bottom. Within a short while the monkey was back and this time the man asked him to do the ironing, which he finished quickly. This went on and on – and soon the householder began to run out of tasks. The monkey was all over him, harassing him and demanding to be given his next duty.

The householder was at his wits' end and decided to consult the wise man once again. Having taken the wise man's advice on board, the householder returned home and asked the monkey to dig a hole in the backyard. This was done in a flash and the monkey was back. The householder then asked the monkey to cut down a long bamboo pole and plant it upright in the hole. Again, this was done in a flash. The householder told the monkey that, when there were no other tasks to be done, his remaining task would be to climb up and down the pole. Soon the monkey was clambering up and down it – and within a short while lay in an exhausted heap at the bottom of the pole, leaving the householder to enjoy the peace and quiet of his home.

As these traditional stories go, they are typically quite simple, yet very profound. The monkey represents the *mind*, which is always moving. That is its nature, always wanting to be active. When it has not been given something to do it will start doing its own thing and, in the absence of something constructive to focus on, the mind tends to run wild.

What the mind does when running amok will depend on what has been programmed into our individual *acquired nature*. The mind is usually conditioned to think up all sorts of things about the past and the future that rarely have any relevance to what is going on in the present. While we are often unaware of our *conditioned thinking*, it nevertheless has an effect on us, which is to distract and undermine us.

The wise man in the story is the inner sage or conscious observer, who helps the householder, the *ego-identity*, to bring the monkey-mind to a point of focus and stillness by giving it something constructive to do. The mind, when connected with the senses under the power of our conscious attention, is brought to a point of focus and stillness, creating a heightened state of readiness for action.

When the monkey-mind is brought under the authority of the inner sage, a transition is made from a *moving, distracted mind* to a *still, focused mind* – and the confidence that follows is inevitable. The bottom line is that we have a *choice*: we can either live under the tyranny of the monkey-mind or we can live with increased freedom and choice under the direction of the conscious observer.

**Analogy: Executive Director**

When the monkey-mind has the liberty to run about unchecked, it takes over the system and attempts to run the show. It's a bit like having a junior manager take over a corporation – no offence to junior staff intended! The best way to run a corporation is to have the executive director running the show, with the broader perspective that goes with that role.

**The Nature of the Senses**

To understand how the practice of conscious awareness works, we also need to understand the nature of our five senses. The way in which I help clients understand the nature of the senses is to ask them to humour a seemingly unusual line of enquiry for a moment. It is interesting that nobody ever says 'no' – we're so polite.

This line of enquiry begins with the question, 'What is your favourite song?' Having identified a song, I'll then ask, 'Can you hear that song right now?' Most will say that they can and I'll ask, 'Are you remembering the song and hearing it in the mind, or are you actually hearing it through your sense of hearing?' With that they usually get the idea and the answer is 'no'. I then ask, 'What's your favourite meal?' and 'Can you taste that meal presently?' If appropriate, we'll work through examples with the other senses as well. Having gone through this process, I'll then ask, 'What does this tell us about our senses?'

Nature of Our Five Senses

Figure 27

The reality is that our senses *only operate in the present*. Our five senses are bound by natural laws to function only in the present moment (see Figure 27). We cannot actually *hear* our favourite song if that song is not being played here and now. We might be able to remember the song and 'hear' it over and over in our mind. Because the mind is such a powerful instrument, we might be able to recall every note, but this occurs only through the act of remembrance. If the song is not being played we simply cannot hear it. The senses only operate in the present.

> 'Our five senses are bound by natural laws to function only in the present.'

In contrast, the habitual pseudo-thinking of the monkey-mind is about what has happened in the past and what might happen in the future. Both of which we can do precious little about. We tend not to think about the present as that is known to us – and we only really start thinking when we do not know something. In this way, the monkey-mind hijacks the system and carries us away in unintentional pseudo-thinking.

To go off on a tangent, absentmindedly thinking about the past and the future, is to take ourselves away from the *moment-of-impact*. As we have seen through practising conscious awareness, the way to re-engage with the present is by *connecting the mind to the senses*. Because the senses are bound by the laws of nature to operate in the present, when connected to the senses, the mind comes into the present. With this we enter a *heightened state of readiness* and, like a cat stalking an unsuspecting bird, we are ready to spring into action. Compared to the sort of action that follows from having a distracted mind, action that follows from a poised, still and present mind is full of potentiality.

> 'Because the senses are bound by the laws of nature to operate in the present, when connected to the senses, the mind comes into the present.'

### The Power of Conscious Attention

Essential to the practice that we've been considering is the power inherent in our conscious attention. Attention is essentially the alignment of our inner faculties through our conscious awareness.

When our faculties are aligned and active, they perform efficiently and effectively.

The conduit for conscious awareness is our faculty of attention. *What we give attention to will grow*. If we give our attention to the voice of doubt, that voice will feed on our hijacked consciousness and dominate our performance potential. When we withdraw our attention from doubt, and connect with the real world, we enter a heightened state of readiness.

> 'The conduit for conscious awareness is our faculty of attention.'

> **Observation: Limited Doubt vs. Limitless Consciousness**
>
> When people describe situations to me in which they've been consumed by doubt, such as before presenting or another challenging event, they often state that as soon as they start their anxiety diminishes and only re-surfaces when they think about it again and thereby give it their attention.
>
> The laws of nature are such that doubt *cannot exist* without the power of conscious attention. As soon as our attention is withdrawn, the doubt disappears. As soon as the presenter begins presenting, his attention is withdrawn from the doubt and connected to the presentation. In so doing, the presenter is no longer attending to the doubt and consequently it disappears.

A cornerstone of accessing confidence in the Stretch Zone is found in our *faculty of attention*, through which our consciousness is channelled. While consciousness is permanent, our attention is impermanent, coming and going depending on our inner state. That is the challenge – to bring our attention under the authority of the *sage* within.

**Hidden in our Language**

While what is being described here might seem unusual, the connection between our senses and our attention is actually a more familiar concept than we might at first think. It is even reflected in our language. How often do we describe someone as being *senseless*? We say that 'he's lost his senses' or that 'she needs to come to her senses'. This is exactly in keeping with what we have been discussing here – when the mind and senses are disconnected and we drift off on to autopilot under the tyranny of the monkey-mind and inner idiot. On the other hand, someone who is making a lot of sense might be described as being 'sensible', as in *sense-able*.

Similarly, the notion of being *absent-minded* implies that the mind is absent from the present. We often speak of the 'absent-minded professor' who cannot find his glasses, which are perched on top of his head. We also talk about someone being a 'scatterbrain', which implies that the mind is all over the place.

The practice of conscious awareness is nothing new and yet, paradoxically, it is entirely new every time it is put into practice. This is a universal form of knowledge that is applicable to everyone, everywhere, always.

**In Summary**

1. To understand the impact of practising conscious awareness we need to understand the nature of the mind, senses and attention.

2. The nature of the mind is to move, yet it moves predominantly on autopilot.

3. The senses are such that they are bound by the laws of nature to function only in the present.

4. Our faculty of attention is the conduit of our consciousness: it conducts consciousness.

5. When connected to our senses through our attention, our minds are bound by the laws of nature to engage with the present moment.

## 43. Further Techniques in Being Confident

While the foundation practice of conscious awareness provides a panacea that is universally applicable to anyone, anywhere, anytime, it can also be adapted into a variety of different forms. Essentially the different techniques are one and the same, creating the conditions that are conducive to our *being confident*.

---

**Key Question:**

With respect to the practice of conscious awareness, what other similar exercises have you come across within your own experience?

---

The foundation practice is the bedrock upon which the techniques that follow are based. The practice of conscious awareness can be performed once or twice a day or whenever it comes to mind, for a half-minute or one or two minutes, depending on what feels appropriate. The idea is not to force the practice, but to practise light-heartedly, with a spirit of genuine enquiry.

The foundation practice can be adapted as follows:

### 1. Pause to Connect

Pause to connect is about pausing during life's hustle and bustle and re-connecting with conscious presence. The only difference to the foundation practice is that we connect to only one of our senses rather than all five. This can be done whenever we spot we're on autopilot.

The practice involves connecting the mind and senses, bringing the monkey-mind to poised focus and stillness. Which of the five senses you re-connect with is entirely up to you. You might prefer to vary it or consistently re-connect with the same sense. My favourites are hearing and touch; however, I do use them all at different times.

### 2. Connected Attention

Connected attention is about maintaining conscious awareness in action. While the foundation practice is about connecting mind and senses in a moment that is specially put aside for that purpose, connected attention is about focusing our attention on what we are doing here and now – at the *moment-of-impact*. When our conscious attention is kept on the activity itself, the monkey-mind cannot go off on tangents.

For example, when walking to a meeting, simply be aware of feeling your feet on the ground, and noticing the people and objects around you. When having a difficult conversation, listen fully to the sound of your voice and theirs. Regardless of what you are doing, all you need to do is to connect your attention to your actions and your surroundings through the five senses.

### 3. Conscious Breathing

Conscious breathing is a well known practice whereby you allow your attention to rest on the inhalation and exhalation of your breath. The attention simply rests on the sensation of touch as the air comes and goes through the nostrils. In this practice, there is no need to interfere with the rate and depth of your breathing; you only need to rest your attention on the breathing. This can be an incredibly relaxing practice, balancing your state within.

### 4. Self-Observation

Self-observation is the practice of looking in on yourself from the perspective of the conscious observer, free from any ego-identity. When observing yourself with full attention, you will notice any fear and doubt and can make conscious choices accordingly.

This exercise is not about the geeky teenager-like habit of being self-conscious. It is about conscious observation of yourself in the present. Self-observation doesn't entail 'thinking' about yourself; it is about observing yourself with conscious attention. It is also not about self-criticism, but about observing yourself with detached interest.

> 'Self-observation doesn't entail thinking about yourself; it is about observing yourself with conscious attention.'

### 5. Reflection

Reflection is about stepping back and considering a challenge. It begins with a *pause to connect*, which brings the mind to stillness, and is followed by a deliberate reflection on what is known and what is not known, and so on. You can also put questions to the mind and then deliberately not think of the answer, practising *self-observation* to see what arises.

Rather than 'me' having the answers, when questions are put to that amazing instrument, the mind, answers seem to come of-the-moment without our having to do all the hard work thinking of the answers. Without ego-interference, the answers are so often refreshingly different, yet profoundly simple.

### 6. Remembering Yourself – Forgetting Yourself

This technique is about reminding yourself of the inner sage and your natural confidence by forgetting about the inner idiot that's tangled up with the monkey-mind. To forget is to become disinterested in the inner idiot's misleading comments by becoming interested in and giving your attention to the inner sage's supportive directives in the conscious present.

This technique evokes the relatively common experience whereby we literally forget ourselves for a moment and do something incredible – and then ask ourselves, 'Was that me?' and 'How did I do that?' What happens is that we forget to doubt ourselves and our inner confidence arises naturally. The technique is about taking your attention away from 'thinking' about the inadequate you, and refocusing on the *moment-of-impact* instead.

### 7. Statement of Conscious Intention

This technique is about reminding ourselves that we can. Statements I use personally include 'I am and I can', 'I can do this' or 'you can do this'. In order for this technique to work it needs to be a conscious resolution. However, the resolution is not to achieve a particular result. It is to focus and align your inner resources, holding them in tension, to do the best you can.

In his 2008 election victory speech, President Barack Obama, repeatedly said, 'Yes we can,' and this had a very potent effect. When we remind ourselves that we can, *we can*. This technique is best practised with conscious attention. If not, it is likely to become just another desperate effort to psyche ourselves up.

> 'When we remind ourselves that we can, we can.'

Because it *is* conscious, a statement of conscious intention brings us out of the autopilot-like self-doubt and into conscious presence, with genuine confidence.

### 8. A Question of State?

Another excellent technique is to silently ask yourself: 'What is the condition of my inner state?' This question will remind you that you have a state, which in turn will help to wake you up and bring your faculties into alignment. As soon as you place your state under conscious observation, it will begin to change for the better. You will become aware of what *was* and become open to what *can be*.

---

**Example: Facilitating with Confidence**

The fundamental principle underlying all of these techniques is to *get out of the mind* and into the real world by *connecting the mind and senses* through *conscious attention*.

No matter how many years I have been a facilitator, I still feel nervous before running an event. What I have noticed is that my monkey-mind gets going with questions such as: 'Will I remember what I need to say?' 'Will they like me?' 'Will everything go according to plan?' 'Will there be any nasty people in the group?' And even, 'Will they laugh at my jokes?' These questions arise unintentionally and, if given an inch, will create and re-create a spiral of doubt.

As soon as I become aware of that doubt I *pause to connect*. Nobody needs to know what I am doing. So, standing there in the training room, I consciously feel my feet on the floor, hear the sounds round about, and so on. I'll then set up the room, moving chairs about and, at the same time, practising *connected attention*, feeling the weight of the chair as I lift it, noticing where I want it to be, for instance. While preparing some flipcharts, I'll give my attention to the writing, colours and spaces.

---

When attending in this way, 'the doubt cannot creep in', as Helen once put it to me. Our doubt might butt its head in every now and then, but as soon as it does and we observe it doing so, it is butted out immediately. The more this process is practised, the easier it becomes until it is second nature to us.

As participants arrive for the event, I'll approach each person in turn and consciously greet them, welcoming them to the programme. Finally, just before the programme starts, I'll find a quiet spot and *pause to connect*. In so doing, the programme begins from a place of conscious awareness for me, which is the best place to start any activity. Whenever I practise the techniques described, my doubt cannot creep in and my confidence comes through naturally.

During a final coaching session with Siofra, we discussed the benefits of the practice. 'It has definitely helped,' she said, adding, 'It immediately grounds you.' She went on to say that while 'the old me would have been getting tied up in knots', the practice 'helps you to deal with whatever comes up rather than try to second guess and get worked up'.

Siofra described her increased feelings of confidence, saying, 'You don't have to do anything, it comes naturally,' and revealing, 'I am consciously not thinking things through before I speak,' Having been promoted at the time, she confirmed, 'I feel incredibly in control and really relaxed'. And she concluded, 'I probably haven't truly believed in myself until now'.

### In Summary

1. Supporting the foundation practice is a variety of alternative techniques.

2. The critical factor with each technique is that it entails our coming out of autopilot into the present.

3. Because the techniques are subtle, no one needs to know that you are practising them.

## 44. Secondary Techniques from the Outside In

In support of the primary techniques which work from the *inside out* are several secondary techniques that work from the *outside in*. When used in conjunction with the primary techniques, these secondary techniques can help build our feeling of confidence.

---

**Key Question:**

What do you think makes the secondary techniques more effective when used in support of the primary practices?

---

While there are many secondary techniques, we'll focus on the following six. The purpose of this section is not to provide a definitive exposition of these techniques but rather to raise your awareness of them and hopefully whet your appetite for further exploration.

### 1. Goal Setting

As a species, human beings seem to be happiest and at their productive best when they have a clear sense of purpose. Goals provide a means whereby we can work our way towards our purpose through bite-sized chunks. Every time we achieve a goal the feeling of achievement boosts our confidence. It's that sweet taste of success!

---

'Goals provide a means whereby we can work our way towards our purpose through bite-sized chunks.'

---

Setting goals creates a pathway for regular achievement against which we can track our progress. When setting goals, the trick is to set goals that are realistic, balancing our capacity to stretch ourselves against our goals' achievability. When too easy, goals will not inspire us. When too difficult, goals can even undermine us.

However, if your goals are formulated correctly, you'll know exactly what you need to achieve and by when. Once you've set them, avoid distractions and follow through with conscious intention.

Unfortunately, our best intentions seldom become actual realities because we quickly revert back to autopilot, in which state our goals often become no more than a distant memory. Well set goals which are empowered by our conscious attention are simply that much more likely to be achieved.

## 2. Self-Coaching

Working with a coach who is objective and detached can provide a powerful means to help you engage with your aspirations and the challenges you may meet along the way. Self-coaching is exactly the same thing, with the only difference that you need to be both coach and client.

Given all that's been said about the inner sage and conscious observer, it's probably no surprise to learn that we each have a built-in coach, who is in a prime position to support us in our challenges and aspirations. As self-coach, a key practice is to ask yourself lots of challenging questions that make you stop, think and see your situation from a wider, more objective perspective. These sorts of questions include:

- What happened in that performance?

- What effect did that have?

- What worked well?

- What did not work well?

- What would I like to do differently?

- How can I improve on what went well?

- What might that have looked like from X's perspective?

- What specifically will I do differently next time?

The trick to self-coaching is to focus on the successes as much as the not-so successes. Questions such as 'what worked really well?' will help you to raise awareness of your strengths, which can really boost your confidence.

### 3. Feedback

While it can be quite intimidating at first, receiving feedback is often a highly rewarding and confidence-boosting experience. What makes the idea of feedback seem intimidating is the irrational idea that our performance was not good enough. Experience has taught me that in every performance there is always something positive to take away – we only have to look for it. So good feedback begins with what worked well.

However, challenging feedback, when delivered effectively, can be just as instructive and confidence boosting. With challenging feedback, we become more aware of what we could have done differently, placing us in a strong position to do better next time.

The trick is not to wait around for someone to give you feedback, but to ask proactively for it. People are usually only too pleased to be asked for their feedback and only too happy to give it. Asking for feedback is an act of confidence in itself.

The worst thing you can do when receiving feedback is to become defensive and argumentative. If defensive and argumentative, you can be sure that your inner idiot has hijacked your inner state and is resisting the feedback. When receiving feedback, all you need to do is to listen fully, thank the person and then explore their observations as appropriate.

### 4. Relationship Building

Another way to build confidence is by developing a good network of genuine relationships. Healthy relationships can provide an excellent source of support when we find ourselves in the Stretch Zone and, when needed, may offer some real, honest and helpful feedback. When we are surrounded by people we trust, their mere presence often has a way of boosting our confidence and performance potential.

Relationships that really make a difference are those that have some depth and meaning, where there is a real resonance and connection. Peripheral relationships can help, but only to a certain degree. Relationships in which all those involved say what they think and mean what they say are the most helpful kind. Within these sorts of relationships, people have real conversations, not necessarily easy conversations, and the underlying trust positively lifts our confidence and potential.

### 5. Knowledge

Many years ago, John Scully, a respected tutor, advised me to 'become an expert in what you do'. When we commit to developing our knowledge and expertise, we will often feel more confident about ourselves. And there is always something more to know. So, in reality, we are never 'an expert', which is frequently just another ego-identity.

Of one thing we can be certain: we're unlikely to ever know everything. Not knowing can be very difficult for some people, even competent experts. However, not knowing is actually perfectly acceptable and there is nothing wrong with saying, 'I don't know, but I'll find out and get back to you.' Being open and direct in that way conveys confidence and credibility in itself.

In the Stretch Zone, we will often find that it is simply not possible to have all the detailed information we'd like to have. If you find yourself in this situation, it is important to prevent yourself being hijacked by fear and doubt, and to be comfortable with the discomfort of not having all the information you might like.

### 6. Humour and Perspective

It is vitally important to keep a sense of perspective and humour towards the challenges we face in life. So often when we lose perspective, we end up making a mountain out of a molehill and blow things completely out of proportion. As soon as you lose your sense of perspective you can bet your bottom dollar that the inner idiot has hijacked your inner state.

Things are seldom as serious as the inner idiot makes out. When things are getting to us, it can be helpful to ask ourselves just how highly our concerns rate against what is really important. When we stand back and put our worst case scenarios into perspective, they mostly come down a few rungs on the ladder of what really is important and what is not important.

There is a wonderful story that captures this so well.

### Getting Your Priorities Right – Jar, Stones, Pebbles and Sand

A philosophy professor stood before his class with some items on the desk in front of him. When the class began, he wordlessly picked up a large empty mayonnaise jar and proceeded to fill it with rocks of about two inches in diameter. He then asked the students if the jar was full. They agreed that it was.

The professor then picked up a box of pebbles and poured them into the jar. He shook the jar lightly. The pebbles, of course, rolled into the open spaces between the rocks. Again, he asked the students if the jar was full. They agreed it was. The students laughed.

The professor picked up a box of sand and poured it into the jar. Of course, the sand filled up everything else. 'Now,' said the professor, 'I want you to recognise that this is your life. The rocks are the important things – your family, your partner, your health, your children – things that if everything else was lost and only they remained, your life would still be full.

'The pebbles are the other things that matter, like your job, your house, your car. The sand is everything else, the small stuff. If you put the sand into the jar first, there is no room for the pebbles or the rocks. The same goes for your life. If you spend all your time and energy on the small stuff, you will never have room for the things that are important to you.

'Pay attention to the things that are critical to your happiness. Play with your children. Take time to get medical checkups. Take your partner out dancing. There will always be time to go to work, clean the house, give a dinner party and fix the disposal. Take care of the rocks first – the things that really matter. Set your priorities. The rest is just sand.'

> But then ... a student took the jar which the other students and the professor agreed was full, and proceeded to pour in a glass of beer. Of course the beer filled the remaining spaces within the jar, making the jar truly full. The moral of this tale is – no matter how full your life is, there is always room for a beer.
>
> Unknown

Every day we need to make sure we're fully aware of what is important and what is not important and act accordingly. So often we think we know what is important and what is not important – and we most likely do – however, because we're on autopilot, within the domain of the inner idiot, we very quickly loose our way and become buried in the sand.

**In Summary**

1. The *secondary techniques* when used in support of the *primary techniques* can be great.

2. Goal setting creates an opportunity to work towards your purpose through bite-size chunks.

3. Self-coaching provides a means to think through your performance by accessing your inner sage.

4. Feedback creates a mirror from which you can learn about your performance potential.

5. A network of relationships can provide a wealth of support and feedback.

6. Become a knowledgeable expert in your field, a point of reference for others.

7. Make sure you discriminate between the rocks, the pebbles and the sand in life.

## 45. Inner and Outer Feedback Loops

While the sort of proactive feedback that we touched upon in the previous chapter is great, we often don't realise that we're getting feedback constantly – whether we like it or not. And this constant supply of feedback has a direct and immediate impact on our confidence and potential.

**Key Question:**

In what ways might you be constantly receiving feedback?

Feedback about ourselves is not an occasional thing, but a constant that comes to us either consciously or unconsciously via two interdependent feedback loops. The *internal feedback loop* is about feedback we give ourselves as we observe the impact we have on others. The *external feedback loop* is the feedback we receive from others in response to our impact on them. While feedback loops are by no means rocket science, their impact on us is substantial.

### Impressions = Feedback

The bottom line is that our speech and actions create an impression – and an impression means feedback. We cannot *not* communicate. We are always making an impression about ourselves, whether we like it or not. That impression is part of a very natural feedback process, either internally or externally, which shapes our confidence and self-esteem.

'We cannot not communicate. We are always making an impression about ourselves, whether we like it or not.'

As creatures of habit, we all have our conditioned behaviours through which we convey impressions about ourselves, yet we are seldom aware of these behaviours or the impressions we create at the time. As people react to us (creating outer feedback) and as we interpret their reactions (inner feedback), we end up criticising ourselves relentlessly. Most self-criticism is a conditioned habit rooted in autopilot.

## Three Channels of Communication

Professor Albert Mehrabian, a psychologist, did some research into the relative impact of three different channels through which we communicate. These are verbal, vocal and visual channels, although Mehrabian did not use these words. The verbal channel refers to *what* we say, the vocal channel refers to *how* we say it and the visual channel refers to how we *look* when we say it, our body language. What Professor Mehrabian found was that the relative impact of the three channels is not what we might assume it to be.

Our typical assumption is that we influence others through *what* we say. However, Professor Mehrabian found it is actually our visual and vocal channels that are most influential. According to his research, the verbal channel only accounts for 7 per cent of our total impact. The vocal and visual channels represent 38 per cent and 55 per cent respectively, with a total of 93 per cent in combination (see Figure 28).

3V Channels of Communication

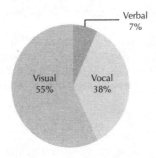

Figure 28        Albert Mehrabian

---

### Example: 'I'm Fine!'

Imagine asking a female acquaintance how she is and that person replies, 'I'm fine.' Should her vocals and visuals convey a congruent message, her verbal response would be easy to accept. However, if her vocals sound irritable and her visuals seem dismissive, you might question what she said verbally.

In fact, the research says that we all give more credence to vocal and visual channels than to vocabulary. If these don't tally with the words, we will come to the conclusion that your friend is not fine. Perhaps the underlying reason behind this is that, while it is easy to manipulate our words, it is not so easy to mask our vocals and visuals.

It is interesting to note that while we trainers often quote these percentages, the actual research was completed with an insignificant research sample that is hardly representative of the general population. This naturally raises questions as to the validity and reliability of the research. However, rather than enter into a whole lot of mental gymnastics about the academics of these findings, we could simply exercise some common sense.

Common sense strongly suggests that we communicate at different levels and derive differing levels of meaning from the three channels, or '3Vs' (a handy way to remember them). If, for example, our visuals and vocals look and sound confident, yet verbally we are talking a load of nonsense, the vocal and visual channels are hardly likely to make much difference to how others interpret what is being said. While the vocal and visual channels are important, the verbal channel provides the baseline from which to work. As to the exact percentages – well, that's just detail.

### Creating a Positive Impression

If our behaviours, in the form of the words we use and how we sound and look when we use them, can have such a direct effect on our impact on others, we need to understand how this process works.

#### a) Verbal Channel: Your Words and Phrases

The importance of the verbal channel cannot be stressed enough. Contrary to the research, in my experience I have found that our words and phrases say a lot about us and significantly affect our impact on others. Aspects to keep in mind include your language, the content of your speech, colloquial speech, jargon, humour and habitual speech mannerisms such as 'err', 'like' or 'umm'.

## b) Vocal Channel: How You Sound

The vocal channel helps to convey the emotion behind your words, conveying much about yourself and your inner state. The following needs to be kept in mind:

- **Tone** – how high or low you speak says a lot about you. A high pitch conveys apprehension. A mono-tone can sound boring. Resonant and varied tones are best.

- **Pace** – if you speak too quickly you will convey anxiety. When too slow, you will come across as tedious and frustrating. A varied and appropriate pace is best.

- **Volume** – when too soft you may sound insecure. If too loud, you could sound arrogant. Volume needs to be appropriate, making it easy to be heard.

- **Inflection** – emphasis in speech influences meaning and impact. To get a sense of this in practice, read the following aloud, emphasising different words: *I did not say he stole the money.*

- **Pause** – if you fill natural gaps in speech and conversation too quickly, this can convey apprehension. A well timed pause conveys poise, presence, a calm confidence.

## c) Visual Channel – Our Body Language

The visual channel says much about your presence and state, and will significantly affect the impression you have on others:

- **Posture** – while an imposing posture conveys arrogance, a slouched posture conveys insecurity. Confidence is best conveyed through an upright and relaxed posture.

- **Gestures** – eager, flighty hand gestures can convey insecurity. Sluggish gestures convey disinterest. Gestures should be balanced and appropriate.

- **Smile** – an overly confident cheesy grin does not work. To convey confidence a smile needs to be authentic, coming from the heart.

- **Eye Contact** – measured eye contact conveys presence and confidence. However, too much comes across as domineering or over eager. Avoidance conveys anxiety.

- **Handshake** – knuckle crunching is out as it conveys insecurity or a desperate attempt to impress. A limp handshake is just as off-putting. Firm and warm is best.

- **Personal Presentation and Dress** – whether it is formal, smart-casual, casual or chilled out, what you wear needs to be both comfortable and appropriate to the occasion.

## Congruent Communication

The ideal verbal, vocal and visual pattern would be impossible to define. What is suggested here is merely a guideline as we each need to find what works best for us. Essential to the impressions we create is the extent to which the three channels are congruent, creating a consistent message and impression.

## Inner Feedback Loop

With regards to the inner feedback loop, there are two things to bear in mind. Firstly, it is not optional and is working almost all the time as we digest our performance and the perceived impressions that we have on others. Secondly, if it is not working consciously, the only other alternative is for it to be working unconsciously. And, when we are on autopilot, the unconscious feedback loop becomes a conditioned opportunity for the inner idiot to start finding fault with everything we do. We are so often our own worst critics.

The trick with the inner feedback loop is *objectivity*. When we view ourselves with increased levels of objectivity, the voice of the inner critic is replaced with more constructive feedback. The best way to become objective is to be emotionally detached – which is what makes feedback from others potentially so powerful.

> 'The trick with the inner feedback loop is objectivity.'

**Example: Music Exam**

As your own worst critic, you may need to remember to focus on the positives in your performance. Having taken an exam in classical guitar, I found myself walking out of the examination room with a head full of self-criticism. I did not feel well that day and played within my capability. As I left the examination room, I started to criticise myself for wasting more than a year's worth of practice.

Walking to my car, I observed the rampant self-criticism. Practising *connected attention*, I stopped it short, giving attention to the feeling of my feet on the pavement as I walked. When in the car, I *paused to connect* and practised some *self-coaching*, asking myself, 'What went well in the examination?' I quickly found that actually a lot had gone really well and I also discovered some learning points that I could take to my next exam. The practices silenced the inner critic in its tracks. As it turned out, I passed!

Feedback is a powerful way to boost your confidence from the *outside in*. Whether internal or external, the benefit is maximised when received with conscious awareness.

**In Summary**

1. *Inner feedback* is the feedback we give ourselves when we observe our impact on others.

2. *Outer feedback* is feedback we receive from others as we make an impression on them.

3. We cannot *not* communicate: we are always making an impression about ourselves to ourselves and others.

4. *Feedback* loops are not optional and are either conscious or unconscious.

## 46. Scratching Below the Surface

When we scratch below the surface, it becomes apparent that an *outside in* approach presents some advantages as well as potential pitfalls. The more we are aware of these two sides to the coin, the more we can make the most of these potentially helpful practices.

---

**Key Question:**

Which pitfalls do you think might be associated with boosting confidence from the *outside in*?

---

Building confidence from the *outside in* not only changes our outer behaviour, it can also influence our inner state. For example, when we focus on projecting our vocals, we focus our attention on the sound of our voice, which means that we are actually taking our attention away from the nagging doubts in our monkey-minds.

Vocals occur in the present, and as soon as we give our attention to our voices in the here and now, we come out of the past and future doubts – and into the present. We have already seen how what we give attention to will grow. If we attend to doubt, it will grow. However, if we attend to the sound of our voice, our presence grows.

It is not the change in our outer behaviours that makes the difference. It is the change that takes place in our own state. When we wake up in the morning feeling down in the dumps, but smile at ourselves in the mirror, it is not the smile that makes the difference. What makes the difference is the inner change that occurs when we take our attention away from our misery and give it to our smile in the present.

There are three key ways in which an *outside in* approach can substantially support the *inside out* approach:

**1. *We Become What We Practise:*** in *Hamlet*, Shakespeare wrote of needing to 'assume a virtue if we have it not'. Mahatma Gandhi said you need to 'be the change you want to see'. As we assume a virtue and *become* the change we want to see in ourselves, the change becomes who we are – it becomes second nature. In fact, it is our *essential nature*.

**2. *Focus for Our Conscious Attention:*** the verbal, vocal and visual channels provide a helpful focus for our attention. The act of listening to the sound of your own voice, for example, takes place in the present, taking you away from nagging doubt and refocusing you in the present moment. This is the practice of *connected attention*.

**3. *Internal and External Feedback Loops:*** when we focus on our verbal, vocal and visuals (as above) our inner and outer feedback loops come into positive effect, lifting our confidence.

The trouble with an *outside in* approach in isolation is that the confidence that follows is unlikely to last. When, in our emotionally hijacked state, we psyche ourselves up by speaking loudly, standing tall and the like, the pseudo-confidence that follows is neither convincing nor sustainable. Consciousness remains the master key.

> 'The trouble with the outside in approach in isolation is that the confidence that follows is unlikely to last.'

When we attend to our verbal, vocal and visual behaviours with conscious intention, our attention goes with it and our state is completely different. When we react out of conditioned habit, our state is no different and, as senior banker Andrew put it to me, when you build confidence on the outside only, 'then you are in danger of building yourself a huge facade'.

### *Inside Out* vs. *Outside In*

Given what has been said, it is clear that the two approaches complement one another. So where is the confidence in all this? Is confidence an upright posture or direct eye contact? Is confidence a hearty vocal projection or smooth haircut? These objects and behaviours are not confidence in and of themselves. So what exactly *is* confidence?

> **Key Point:**
>
> Confidence is that inner state of certainty that you can perform to your potential and deal with things as they arise, fearlessly and without caution or hesitation, free from any inner or outer limitations.

Confidence is an inner state. Confidence is our natural state. Confidence is the absence of doubt. Tone, posture, word choice, facial gestures and such like are behavioural manifestations of confidence, but not the confidence itself. To work on the behaviours alone is to work on the periphery. When we address something on the surface alone, the effect just does not last. The foundations are simply not there to sustain it. Genuine confidence begins from within.

### The Flip Side

On the flip side of the coin, when we interfere with our behaviour by attempting to fake or manufacture our desired ideal behaviours, we run the risk of inadvertently undermining the very confidence we are attempting to develop. An attempt to manufacture the 'right' behaviours is usually a knee-jerk reaction created by our inner idiot and only serves to undermine and distract us.

In contrast, when we change our state and align with the conscious observer, our verbal, vocal and visual behaviours will take care of themselves. In the absence of the doubt in the monkey-mind, our outer behaviours adjust naturally. So there is no need to do anything. Rather than attempting to *have confidence*, all we need to do is to *be confident*.

When our behaviours adjust naturally to our inner conscious state, our verbal, vocal and visuals are authentic and congruent. Not only are the behaviours more convincing; they are also sustainable and the feedback loops that follow reflect this as well.

**In Summary**

1.  Focusing on the 3Vs moves our attention from our doubt to our behaviour in the present.

2.  Our behaviours provide a useful avenue to direct our conscious attention.

3.  Confidence lies not in the behaviours themselves, but in our internal state.

4.  Attempting to manufacture ideal behaviours is typically a knee-jerk reaction – of *having confidence*.

5.  When we are focused in the present, our verbal, vocal and visual behaviours adjust naturally and authentically.

Part Eight
# The Third Principle

## 47. Keeping the Doubt Unlearnt

If confidence is *the absence of doubt* and *our natural state*, it follows that once we become aware of our emotionally and mentally hijacked states and have quietened our doubt, our confidence should re-surface naturally – end of story. Yet this is not always our experience.

---

**Key Question:**

From your experience, what have you observed in relation to being aware or unaware of doubt – and the effect this has on you? Once you have acknowledged doubt, does it ever disappear for good?

---

In my experience, I have found that once we've re-connected with the present moment and brought our doubt under conscious observation, the following period of freedom from nagging doubt is frequently interrupted as doubt resurfaces once more. Even when we have reconnected our minds and senses through one of the practices discussed in Part Seven, doubt nevertheless continues to raise its unwanted head, again and again.

The good news is that each time that this doubt re-surfaces, it seems to lose some of its power and momentum. With practice, we notice doubt with greater and greater ease, and we begin to take it less and less seriously until it becomes no more than an annoying fly that we simply swat away. Eventually, it gets the message and pushes off indefinitely.

So what initially makes doubt return repeatedly in spite of our best intentions?

### Creating and Re-Creating Doubt

To begin with, we need to be absolutely clear that lacking confidence is a self-imposed limitation. As we have seen, while the events that undermined our confidence initially were most likely external, the processes that sustain our doubt are internal. We are the constant creators of our doubt and the low confidence that follows is part of that deal. Doubt exists in our personal, individual worlds, not in the real world that we all share. I cannot stress enough that no one else even knows your doubt exists. It is a *self-imposed limitation*, which you create for yourself.

> 'We are the constant creators of our doubt and the low confidence that follows is part of that deal.'

People sometimes deceive themselves, attributing their doubt to people, objects and events in their environment. As we saw in Chapter 18, what follows is a *victim mentality*, as they wait for the person, object or event that they hold responsible to change, justifying their lack of confidence and initiative in the process.

The recognition that doubt is a self-imposed limitation is actually really good news. It implies we are in the driving seat and, whenever we are in our Stretch Zone, that we can do something about it. The person we stand the greatest chance of influencing is ourselves. The acceptance of doubt as a self-imposed limitation is an important step in the release of real and sustainable confidence.

You might challenge this by arguing that our doubt can have its origins in external circumstances, such as in constant criticism from our parents, for example. Remember Paul, the senior manager we met in Chapter 2, who said his strict upbringing as a child had an impact on his confidence? While a strict upbringing is an external experience, its impact twenty years later is sustained by us, not our parents, which Paul was able to recognise. Many of us seem to create and recreate continually the conditions within which our doubt thrives, although we are hardly aware of this at the time.

> 'Many of us seem to create and recreate continually the conditions within which our doubt thrives, although we are hardly aware of this at the time.'

However, we do need to be careful here and not discount the fact that, for some people, the external conditions that undermine their confidence are still very much a present reality. Nevertheless, I think it's valid to suggest that the majority of us spend a lot of time unconsciously recreating the conditions within which we personally undermine our confidence.

While some play the victim avoiding responsibility and blaming others, I've found that most people are quite happy to take responsibility for their actions; they're just not aware of their impact on themselves. Unfortunately, such conditioned doubt does not always give up and requires consistent self-observation and practice to iron out.

The next few chapters will explore this, enabling you to relinquish your doubt more and more – until it fades into insignificance.

---

**In Summary**

1. Unfortunately, unlearnt doubt does not always stay unlearnt.

2. The more we practise the exercises in Part Seven, the more doubt will lose its power and momentum in our lives.

3. With practice, it is easier to observe our doubt and we take it less seriously.

4. Doubt is a self-imposed limitation which we create and recreate ourselves.

---

## 48. Emotional Attachment and Identification

In order to release our confidence in full measure, we will have to understand what, besides habitual conditioning, it is that makes our doubt resurface time and again. Central to this are the concepts of emotional attachment and identification.

---

**Key Question:**

What do you understand by the terms emotional attachment and identification?

---

Identification and emotional attachment are two primary drivers behind the spiral of fear and doubt and the undermining effect that this spiral has on our confidence and performance potential.

### Understanding Attachment

What is an attachment? How does it work? What effect does it have? Who has the attachment? Where is it? What powers attachments? A clear understanding of what we mean by attachments will help us to observe them and their impact in practice.

Similar to the way in which we physically attach a bulb to a lamp, we attach ourselves at a psychological level to all sorts of objects, people and situations – but we are seldom aware of what is happening or its limiting effect. At a very simple level, this plays out in a training environment where, after a break, people mostly return to 'their chair' and look disgruntled when someone has taken 'my seat'. Without being aware of it, we become attached to something as irrelevant as 'my chair' – and that is one of the easy forms of attachment.

Dictionary.com defines attachment as 'an act of attaching or the state of being attached', or 'a feeling that binds one to a person, thing, cause, ideal or the like'. So an attachment is an action, something that is being done. It is a state of mind and a feeling that has the effect of *binding* us to some object, person or situation. But what has all this got to do with confidence?

Throughout our formative years and beyond we become attached to objects, ideas, thoughts, feelings, beliefs, conceptions and misconceptions, preferences, fears, aversions, likes and dislikes, desires, habits, situations, people, relationships, roles, results, rewards, successes and failures, our comfort zone – and so on and so on. What attachment has to do with confidence is that it is the means by which our *acquired nature* sets fast and undermines everything we think, say and do.

---

**Example: Pregnant Teenager**

If a friend's teenage daughter told us that she was pregnant, it would be a very different experience from the same situation with, say, our own daughter. Our perception of the situation, our ability to think and speak clearly and our emotional state are likely to be very different. With our own daughter, we are more likely to be angry, critical and disappointed. With our friend's daughter, we are far more likely to be calm, understanding, supportive and practical.

---

What makes the difference? The difference is that we are more emotionally attached to our ideas about our own daughter and her situation, than we are to our friend's daughter – and it is our attachment to these ideas that limits us from seeing the former situation more openly and rationally. An attachment is a limitation that impedes our potential.

### Identification and the Ego-Identity

Attachment implies identification with that attachment. The two concepts are practically synonymous. When we become attached to something, we unconsciously identify ourselves with that thing, viewing it as part of who and what we are. As our definition of our self becomes entrenched, our ego-identity is born and it is very difficult to behave outside the binding attachment (see Figure 29).

## Attachment & Identfication

Figure 29

When someone says, 'I am angry,' they are identifying themselves with 'anger'. As long as the identification is maintained, that is what they become: angry. In the process of identifying ourselves with anger, we exclude other emotional states as potential options and consequently seem incapable of anything other than anger. Identification is like drawing a tiny circle around yourself and that circle becomes the sum of who and what you are. Anything outside the circle becomes an unlikely option.

Confidence is inextricably linked to attachment and identification. 'I am not confident' is a statement of our ego-identity. As soon as we identify with the idea that 'I am not confident' or 'I am only confident under certain circumstances', confidence becomes a near impossibility for us.

> 'Confidence is inextricably linked to attachment and identification.'

### Example: Speaking Up in a Group

Following unpleasant experiences, some people lose confidence in their ability to speak out in a group. The ego-identity that results is: 'I cannot speak out in a group.' Every time the opportunity arises, that aspect of the ego-identity is triggered and the individual freezes, retreating into his comfort zone. Because of attachment and identification, it becomes entrenched in his *acquired nature* and speaking out in a group becomes a real challenge.

## Underlying Power behind our Attachments

To begin to understand identification and attachment, we need to recognise the formidable power they have over us. Happily, with *self-observation* we can easily observe this in practice. When angry, it is very difficult to be happy. When we feel that we are 'right' and others are 'wrong', it is very difficult to be open to other points of view. Similarly, when we feel insecure, it is very difficult to feel confident. Attachments and identification incapacitate wider possibilities. So what makes attachments so powerful?

The power behind our attachments is the underlying emotion upon which they are based. Our attachments are *emotionally charged* limitations, which are constantly ready to trigger whenever the conditions are propitious. Our emotions move us – which is why it's fitting that the word 'motion' is part of the word 'emotion'. They move us in the direction of the attachment and we find ourselves compelled to follow the attachment, even against our best intentions.

> 'The power behind our attachments is the underlying emotion upon which they are based.'

As our attachments and their emotional charge become more and more entrenched within our *acquired nature*s, it becomes 'natural' for us to think, act or speak in a way that is consistent with the attachment. So our behaviour becomes *conditioned by our attachments* and the ideas that support them.

## Diverse Forms of Emotional Attachment

While we seem to be capable of becoming attached to just about anything, there are a few attachments that are particularly worth observing.

*1. Threatening Situations:* bizarre as it might sound, we actually become highly attached to the circumstances that undermine our confidence most. The threatening situation quickly becomes 'my nemesis'; for example, we'll tell others with great conviction that, 'I'm no good in front of a group of senior managers.'

**2. Ego-Identity:** perhaps what we become most attached to is an idea such as, 'I'm not confident' or 'I am only confident in certain circumstances'. The extent and power underlying the ego-identity is formidable – and yet we never pause to question it.

**3. Coping Mechanism:** we also become emotionally attached to our coping mechanisms of *flight* or *fight* as they 'help' us deal with threatening situations. That is why we become so attached to an idea such as 'I need to psyche myself up'.

**4. Desired Results:** as mentioned previously, our attachment to what 'I want' creates a huge amount of performance pressure, which undermines our confidence and potential.

**5. Comfort Zone:** our emotional attachment to our comfort zone is substantial. And we do all that we can to cling to it, even against our best intentions.

As intelligent beings, why do we allow attachments to dominate us unnecessarily? Firstly, it happens very slowly, over years and years, so we hardly notice the change. It also happens to everyone else, so it does not seem unusual – it seems normal. Thirdly, it happens below our conscious awareness. Spending so much time on autopilot, we are largely unaware of what is happening. We might recognise it in retrospect, but it is not so easy to see at the time.

---

**In Summary**

1.  Attachment is an emotionally charged activity that binds us to some object, action or the like.

2.  With attachment, the *ego-identity* emerges out of our identification with that attachment.

3.  Attachment and identification are self-imposed limitations that restrict possibilities.

4.  The power behind our attachments is the underlying emotion upon which they are based.

5.  Attachments happen virtually to all of us and yet we are seldom aware of their existence and impact.

---

## 49. Principle Three: Confidence as Detached Interest

While writing about confidence as *the absence of doubt* and *the natural state*, it became apparent to me that something was missing: a third principle. While not specifically highlighted in my coaching work, this third principle was an important part of my conversations with clients nonetheless. The third principle is the non-stick, Teflon principle of *confidence as detached interest* (see Figure 30).

**Key Question:**

What does *confidence as detached interest* mean to you?

Confidence as Detached Interest

Figure 30

The principles of *confidence as the absence of doubt* and *our natural state* each relate to *thinking* and *nature* respectively. While each of these perspectives plays a critical part in either undermining or releasing confidence, there is another point of view.

What is missing is an *emotional* element. So, with this in mind, just what are emotions? How do they work? What effect do they have? Where do they come from? How do they arise? Who experiences the emotion? To what extent do we need to be subject to our emotional states? How can we manage our emotions effectively? How can we harness the transformative power inherent within our emotional states? And how can we deal better with less helpful emotions?

## Confidence – An Emotive Perspective

Throughout our formative years, and in adult life, we will inevitably find ourselves in the Stretch Zone facing situations that undermine our confidence. As children, most of us tend to bounce back from minor upsets like steel springs, continuing as if nothing happened. Children seem to have a natural resilience that helps them cope with adversity. Should such challenging situations persist, however, the idea that 'I am not confident' will be reinforced and slowly but surely become entrenched in our *acquired nature*.

With repetition, our internalised fear and doubt are taken as certainties, as the truth about who and what 'I am'. In this way the ego-identity is born, a conviction to which we are emotionally attached. Just as a steel spring that is stretched too far for too long loses its springiness, so we lose our resilience and ability to bounce back.

## Non-Attachment – An Alternative Paradigm

If attachments are emotionally charged limitations, the alternative is obviously *non-attachment*, the opposite. So what do we mean by non-attachment? How does this work? If an attachment is an emotionally charged state of being attached to something, then non-attachment must be a state of being unattached and free from the emotional hooks that accompany our attachments. Without the attachment and the accompanying emotional pull, we enjoy freedom of choice, a sense of autonomy. As opposed to mindlessly following *unconscious conditioned attachments*, non-attachment enables *conscious choice*.

> 'As opposed to mindlessly following unconscious conditioned attachments, non-attachment enables conscious choice.'

While many of us seem to know something already about our attachments, non-attachment is seemingly less familiar to us – yet there is an intuitive understanding. If attachments are what limit and bind us to certain conditioned ideas and behaviours, then freedom from these limitations must necessarily be non-attachment.

In order to understand non-attachment, observe little children at play. The reason little children enjoy such freedom, spontaneity, confidence, fearlessness, happiness and creativity is that they have very few attachments with which to limit themselves. They simply have not had the time to build up a repertoire of attachments with which to identify themselves.

As we considered in Chapter 24, a little child does not usually feel attached to preconceived ideas about singing in front of people. A child will just give it a go. He or she is unlikely to have any expectations about how well the performance will go, or harbour fears of being rejected. Children enjoy a tremendous freedom from the sorts of self-imposed limitations that accompany our adult attachments. So what does this have to do with releasing confidence in the Stretch Zone?

Firstly, we need to *recognise* that attachments limit confidence and potential. Secondly, we need to *observe* the attachments as they arise and take hold within us. Thirdly, we need to simply *let go* of the attachment, freeing ourselves to think, speak or act in the ways in which we would like to think, speak or act. This is about *letting go* of our ideas, assumptions and misconceptions through the principle of *confidence as detached interest*.

### The Principle of Detached Interest

Confidence as detached interest provides an antidote for the attachments and identifications that limit us. So what is detached interest and how does it work? Detached interest is a state characterised by an absence of attachment to, or identification with, any object, person or situation, without any loss of genuine interest in that object, person or situation. Detached interest is a primary enabler of genuine self-mastery and releases confidence naturally from within. So let's explore this further.

> 'Detached interest is a primary enabler of genuine self-mastery and releases confidence from within.'

By detached, we mean that state of being free from attachments, of being able to make conscious choices about our thoughts, speech and actions. Within this detached state we are not under the spell of an emotional pull towards conditioned ideas or behaviours. We are free to move this way or that without self-imposed pushing or pulling in any conditioned direction. With detached interest, we are in a heightened *state of readiness* to meet whatever arises, with all our faculties aligned to the effort.

When detached, we enjoy a statesman-like poise, composure and integrity that is not swayed this way or that depending on the whim of our attachments. We also enjoy an increased capacity to see things as they are and not through the tinted glasses of selective perception. And because the mind is poised and our faculties aligned, we are ready to pounce into action with great dexterity and spontaneity. When detached, we are fully engaged in the present – the *moment-of-impact* – and our performance potential is inevitable, even in the Stretch Zone.

### Example: Training Facilitator

Some years ago, during a leadership programme, one of the participants threw a whopping temper tantrum which was aimed specifically at me as the group facilitator. He became worked up about several things relating to the logistics of the programme, over which I had no control. In this particular instance, I was able to say to him calmly and confidently, 'Thank you for being so direct, open and honest …' and I moved the conversation forward without getting caught up in the conflict.

So what makes it relatively easy for me to handle difficult situations at work, whereas at home with my wife I so often put my foot in my mouth? Emotional detachment, that's what!

If confidence is that 'inner state of certainty that you can perform to your potential and deal with things as they arise, fearlessly and without caution or hesitation, free from any inner or outer limitations', then detached interest is the only sustainable way forward.

**In Summary**

1. Repeated exposure to undermining situations drains our natural resilience.

2. With repetition, fear and doubt are internalised and taken as the truth about who we are.

3. Non-attachment is to be free from the emotional hooks that accompany our attachments.

4. Detachment enables conscious choice – freedom from mindless conditioned attachments.

5. Detached interest is the antidote for our self-imposed attachments.

## 50. Detached *with Interest*

The concept of being detached often conjures up ideas of indifference, disinterest and a lack of concern. However, when we approach any endeavour with indifference, we stand precious little chance of success. Indifference is most certainly not what is meant by detached interest.

> **Key Question:**
>
> What, if anything, does indifference have to do with detached interest?

Without genuine *interest*, our chances of making a positive impact on any situation – not to mention a particularly challenging situation – are not that great. Yet, through a lack of understanding, we so often associate detachment with indifference, disinterest and a couldn't-care-less attitude; and yet nothing could be further from the truth.

> 'We so often associate detachment with indifference, disinterest and a couldn't-care-less attitude; and yet nothing could be further from the truth.'

In our modern world, we emphasise passion, being involved, engaged and caring – and the very idea of being detached seems to go against the grain. So what makes detached interest such a powerful friend in releasing confidence and our potential?

### Understanding Detached Interest

Detached interest means that while we are detached, we remain *highly interested* in what is going on at the *moment-of-impact*. In fact, when we have detached interest we are actually more engaged in what is really happening than we are through our attachments. Our attachments mean that we are more interested in, and distracted by, our preferences about *what we want to be happening* than in *what is actually happening*. To be hijacked by the thoughts and emotions associated with our preferences is to undermine our capacity to perform in the Stretch Zone.

Detached WITH Interest

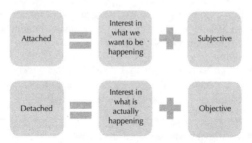

Figure 31

Detached interest does not imply an absence of *preference or intention* and does not exclude setting *goals and objectives*, or pursuing these with determined effort. While you would certainly still set goals, you would simply *not be attached* to them. The difference is subtle but substantial. With detachment, we are in an increased state of readiness to see things as they are and focus our resources where it matters most. And, when we optimise our performance potential in the present, the results take care of themselves (see Figure 31).

When attached to goals, on the other hand, we become emotionally involved with them and identify ourselves with them. Our attention follows the attachment and becomes tangled up in the goal. With our *attention split* between the goal and the performance upon which the goal depends, we are unlikely to reach our potential.

Approaching performance goals with detached interest means that our conscious effort is on the *moment-of-impact* and not on a preoccupation with the desired result in the future. While the goal is only a *potential future reality*, be it in two minutes or two days' time, the performance is an *actual present reality*. The goal is in the future; the performance is in the present.

'While the goal is only a potential future reality, the performance is an actual present reality.'

With detached interest, the goal is most certainly there, but is secondary. What comes first is the performance and our attention follows this priority. While results cannot be guaranteed, the *heightened state of readiness* that accompanies detached interest increases our likelihood of success.

It is important to remember that attachments are not limited to goals and objectives. We seem to have acquired an ability to become emotionally attached to just about anything.

---

### Example: Impact with Senior Executives

While writing this book I had the pleasure of coaching James, a senior leader in the financial services, who had just taken a significant step up the career ladder. And the pressure was on him to make a positive impact right from the start. What James was struggling with was an attachment to the idea that he was not confident with executives. This scenario comes up with surprising frequency with leaders in an organisational context.

When working with clients, colleagues and staff, James was confident in full measure. With executives, however, his attachment to the idea was triggered and his confidence would drop accordingly. All sorts of fears and doubts would surface in the lead-up to a meeting, for example, and this would distract his focus and drain his energy. By the time he arrived at the meeting, he would not be in his usual self-assured state and this would leak out in the meeting. James would end up over doing it by trying too hard. And, as his impact diminished, it would only reinforce his ego-identity's belief, 'I am not confident with executives' – and the attachment would entrench further and further.

As our coaching proceeded, James developed his capacity to observe the attachment from the detached perspective of the conscious observer. He was able to appreciate that the attachment was a completely irrational, self-imposed fiction. Observing the attachment, James was able to *let it go* by coming into the present, at the *moment-of-impact*. When James's attention was focused in the present, his attachment diminished accordingly.

---

Our attachments to our goals, fears, comfort zones and the like hold us back. The next chapter will explore how to let them go and perform with confidence and to our potential.

---

**In Summary**

1.  Detachment is often erroneously associated with indifference or dispassion.

2.  When detached, we are actually more concerned and interested in the present moment than when attached.

3.  With detached interest, we connect with things *as they are*, not as we'd like them to be.

---

## 51. Practising Detached Interest

As we have seen, *confidence as detached interest* provides the antidote to the attachments and identifications through which our fears and doubts become entrenched. What remains is for us to clarify how to put detached interest into practice, in the Stretch Zone when it really matters.

> **Key Question:**
>
> What effect would the exercise in conscious awareness have on our attachments?

The good news is that the practices that enable *confidence as detached interest* are no different from the practices that enable *confidence as the absence of doubt* and *confidence as the natural state*. The exercise in conscious awareness and all its various forms provide the means by which we can transform our state and untangle ourselves from our attachments and ego-identities. Consciousness is the master key upon which everything else depends. Even in the Stretch Zone.

> 'Consciousness is the master key upon which everything else depends.'

### An Unconscious Feeding Frenzy

First and foremost, it's worth noting that our attachments and identifications are internalised unconsciously. It would be ridiculous to say that we make conscious decisions to limit ourselves unnecessarily. Not only are attachments internalised unconsciously, they also thrive in that less-than-conscious state.

When we are emotionally and mentally hijacked while on autopilot, our fear feeds our doubt and the doubt feeds the fear in an unconscious feeding frenzy. The monkey-mind runs riot and the inner idiot takes over our hijacked state – but we are hardly, if ever, aware of our predicament at the time. We take our outcast state as fact, a truth about who we are, entrenching our attachments and ego-identities further and further.

> 'When we are emotionally and mentally hijacked while on autopilot, our fear feeds our doubt and the doubt feeds the fear in an unconscious feeding frenzy.'

Our attachments are conceived within our hijacked state, sustained within that state and will continue to limit within that hijacked state. Yet, we have another choice.

### Knowledge and Awareness – A Double-Edged Sword

Attachments and identifications are best cut asunder with the double-edged sword of knowledge and awareness. While the metaphor of a 'double-edged sword' is typically used in a negative sense, I'd like you to imagine, literally, a bright blade with two sharp edges that can cut sharply in both directions.

An attachment is an activity within us, an activity that is dependent on the feeding frenzy of fear and doubt within our hijacked state. As soon as the 'thinking' and 'feeling' are stopped, the attachment disappears into the nothingness from which it came – our fictional world within. In the absence of the activities that sustain them, our attachments cannot survive. *Awareness* of our fear, doubts and attachments in the present brings about a change in our state, dissolving our attachments in the process.

> 'In the absence of the activities that sustain them, our attachments cannot survive.'

Working alongside this is the *knowledge* that we are not our limiting ego-identities. The statement 'I am not a confident person' is completely false. We need never believe it and impose it on ourselves again. What remains is 'I am' – pure existence which is full of potentiality.

How to wield the double-edged sword can be summed up in the following steps:

- **Observation:** observe your fears, doubts, attachments and ego-identities whenever they attempt to raise their unwanted heads. This is the practice of self-observation.

- **Recognition:** recognise that the ego-identity's claim that 'I am not confident' is completely false. In truth, 'I am' a conscious being with the power of conscious choice.

- **Letting Go:** let go of your attachments immediately by giving your attention to something constructive in the conscious present. This is the practice of connected attention.

Should the attachments re-surface, all you need to do is to return to the present again and again. With tenacious practice, the inner conditioning will fade into insignificance.

### Letting Go and Acceptance

Letting go of fear and doubt is neither to deny nor suppress them. Denial and suppression would mean fighting fear and doubt – and that is exactly what they thrive on, the battle within. Do not make the mistake of thinking that you can defeat them at their own game.

Letting go is about acceptance and disinterest. We firstly need to accept that fear and doubt are there as self-imposed fictions. We then need to become completely disinterested in them by paying them no heed whatsoever and by giving our attention to something constructive in the present. The focus is external rather than internal, on the real world and not on the battle within our private world. In the absence of our conscious energy, fear, doubt, our attachments and identifications cannot survive – they are completely powerless.

When we *observe*, *recognise* and *let go* of fear and doubt, masses of energy previously consumed by the battle within us becomes available to us again. Through the stewardship of our inner sage, this energy can be channelled into something constructive. Channel that energy by focusing your attention on something else at the *moment-of-impact*.

### Unrealistic Expectations – A Word of Caution

When writing the above, I was struck again by the power that underlies our attachments and the extent to which those attachments dominate our lives. Unrealistic expectations that we'll immediately be able to transcend them are not helpful. To set our heart on such unrealistic expectations is to create fresh attachments to new results, which will only serve to limit us in much the same way. The key is to observe our attachments and let them go, channelling our attention within the *moment-of-impact*.

This is a continual process that, with practice, becomes natural. It is, in fact, already natural and all we have to do is stop practising what *seems* natural – i.e. clinging to our attachments – but which is in fact limited and habitual.

---

**In Summary**

1.  In our emotionally hijacked state, fear and doubt feed each other in an unconscious feeding frenzy.

2.  Fear, doubt, attachments and identifications cannot exist in the conscious present.

3.  Whenever we observe them, we need to let go of our attachments and ego-identities.

4.  Letting go is not to deny and suppress them, but to accept and become disinterested in them.

5.  In the absence of the battle within, an abundance of energy becomes available from within us.

---

Part Nine
# Confidence for Everyone

## 52. Seven Patterns of Self-Limiting Doubt

The premise underlying this book is that confidence is our *natural state* and that what undermines this natural state is the prevalence of *doubt in our minds*. In order to unlearn that doubt, it is helpful to improve our understanding about the content of it – of *what* it is that we doubt about ourselves.

---

**Key Question:**

When you are in your Stretch Zone, *what* do your doubts tend to dwell on the most?

---

Given our diverse personalities and life-experiences, we are typically more susceptible to doubting ourselves in our own individual ways. Doubt seems to take on different patterns in different people, or in the same people at different times. These patterns are usually repetitive and predictable and, once understood, are easier to observe in the Stretch Zone.

---

'Doubt seems to take on different patterns in different people, or in the same people at different times.'

---

The patterns as outlined here are not exhaustive, merely a guide to assist your own observations. Essentially, it is *that* we doubt – the act – which is important, not so much *what* we doubt – the content. However, the more we understand the nature of our own doubt, the easier it is to recognise and let go of it in practice. The next section outlines seven forms of doubt and how to deal with them in practice, based on the techniques we studied in Part Seven.

### 1. Doubt about Goals

Confidence is so often undermined by our doubts about the goals we hope to achieve. At the heart of this is the fear that we will fail to achieve what we want to achieve. Our inner idiot and monkey-mind become preoccupied with our attachment to what we want, distracting our focus away from that which leads to the achievement. When our faculties are divided between the goal and the execution of the action that leads to the goal, confidence and success are unlikely.

What makes this form of doubt so powerful is our emotional attachment to our goals. Our attachment not only divides our faculties, it also creates unnecessary pressure to achieve the goal, which in turn only exacerbates our fear and doubt. What follows is either a *flight* reaction as we give up and avoid the situation, or a *fight* reaction as we go in for the kill.

> 'What makes this pattern so powerful is our emotional attachment to our goals.'

Doubt about goals is best dealt with through *focused performance*. Like any other form of doubt, dealing with this pattern begins with *awareness*, observing the doubt and its effect through self-observation, combined with the *knowledge* that it adds no value to the situation whatsoever. The practice of *connected attention* focuses us on the performance, not the doubt. A *statement of positive and conscious intent* to the tune of 'I can do this' goes a long way as well. These practices will help to create a shift in our state and our confidence will release naturally.

### 2. Doubt about Ability

Related to the above is negative thinking about our ability to perform. Here, our doubt is not so much about the outcome, but about the performance that leads to the outcome. At the heart of this form of doubt is the fear that 'I am not good enough', which distracts focus and exacerbates the fear and doubt even further.

What makes doubt about our ability so powerful is that our negative thinking about our ability undermines our ability itself. When we attempt to boost our ability we tend to 'think' about it and this negative, autopilot-like pseudo-thinking only serves to distract.

> 'What makes doubt about our ability so powerful is that our negative thinking about our ability undermines our ability itself'.

Doubt about ability is best dealt with through *curious exploration*. Rather than attempt to anticipate our performance in our imagination, the best thing is to just get started and find out in reality. *Remembering yourself – forgetting yourself* will help you to overcome your negative thinking by stepping off 'planet me'. The technique *pause to connect* also helps to bring the monkey-mind to focused attention.

### 3. Doubt about Knowledge

A highly prevalent form of doubt relates to the extent of our knowledge of a particular subject or situation. At the heart of this is the fear of not knowing, of being exposed with insufficient knowledge. Avoidance so often follows in these situations, as we procrastinate and put things off until we feel we are sufficiently prepared. Yet, within our mentally hijacked state, we never feel adequately prepared.

What makes doubt about knowledge so powerful is that our subsequent avoidance makes us feel even more inadequate, justifying our lack of knowledge even further. So often, our professed need for more detailed information is a means to rationalise an avoidance strategy. A need for lots of information frequently masks a fear of the unknown and of having to deal with the unexpected.

> 'A need for lots of information frequently masks a fear of the unknown and of having to deal with the unexpected.'

People who doubt their knowledge are usually detail orientated and self-critical. For them, not knowing is just intolerable, a very poor reflection of oneself. The drive to have all the bases covered puts them under a lot of unnecessary pressure, which exacerbates their doubt and undermines their performance.

In my experience, I have found that as soon as people get started they usually discover that they have more than sufficient knowledge.

Doubt exists in the monkey-mind, not in the knowledge or lack of it. Not knowing is also usually completely acceptable and can be acknowledged without any loss of face in most situations. In fact, the honesty that such an acknowledgement conveys may result in increased perceived credibility and trust. We are human after all.

Doubt about knowledge can be dealt with through *appropriate balance*. Preparation, where possible, is not to be dismissed. When out of measure, however, it becomes an impediment. Such lack of measure usually happens when we are on autopilot, where we are so emotionally attached to the need for information that we cannot see the wood for the trees. In these situations, *pause to connect* and *conscious breathing* will create balance, a state of being centred within ourselves.

### 4. Doubt about Acceptance

Another prevalent form of doubt relates to the extent to which we feel accepted, as many of us question and re-question how we are seen by others. At the heart of this form of doubt is the fear of being rejected. Fearing rejection, we may seek approval and affirmation unnecessarily. When we feel accepted we feel confident. When we don't our confidence drops accordingly.

> 'Fearing rejection, people seek approval and affirmation unnecessarily.'

What makes this form of doubt so incapacitating is that those who have doubts about acceptance are usually people-focused carers whose natural sensitivity makes them question their own value. Their mental and emotional hijacking centres on what they imagine people think about them, yet it tells them nothing about what others really do think. Hesitant and submissive, they are often dismissed by others, especially by dominant, task-focused people. Being sensitive, they are only too quick to pick up on the slightest sign of rejection and their inner idiots are only too happy to trade on this impression.

Doubt about acceptance is dealt with through *genuine self-acceptance*, whereby we accept who we are, as we are, in the present moment. *Self-observation* will enable us to observe our tendency to seek approval and also to detach ourselves from the inner idiot, who is convinced we need it. *Reflection* on the question, 'Do I really need the approval of others?' can really change our state. *Connected attention* takes the focus away from the pseudo-thinking, focusing it on the task at hand instead.

I have found that as soon as typical people-pleasers realise, 'I don't need the approval of others,' their confidence quickly releases from within and they go on to surprise everyone.

### 5. Doubt about Pace

Another form of doubt is the negative thinking that relates to how quickly something is being done. We question whether we are quick enough, or whether we are being too slow and lagging behind. At the heart of this form of doubt is our fear of falling behind and not getting things done quickly enough. Our fear and doubt drive us to go against our natural preferences and speed things up, adding a whole lot of unnecessary pressure to the situation. Working outside our preferences, our performance drops and our inner idiot finds the means to justify our lack of confidence.

> 'At the heart of this form of doubt is our fear of falling behind and not getting things done quickly enough.'

What makes this form of doubt so challenging is that the mental and emotional hijacking exacerbates the perception that we are not quick enough. As we increase the pressure on ourselves, we become more and more distracted with the result that our capacity to perform effectively and efficiently diminishes – and a spiral of fear and doubt follows accordingly.

Doubt about pace can be dealt with through *poised calm*, where we consciously give ourselves the space to perform at the pace that suits us best. This is about giving yourself permission to work at your own pace and not feeling pressured to perform differently. Experience suggests to me that our feeling of being slow is usually an irrational misperception on our own part, with others not even questioning our pace in the first place. *Pause to connect* and *conscious breathing* are both techniques that will help to settle the panic and bring you back to the *moment-of-impact*.

### 6. Doubt about Control

Another challenging pattern of doubt is the negative thinking that arises in relation to our feelings of control over our confidence and the environment within which we need to make an impact. At the heart of this form of doubt is a fear of the unexpected and the fear that our confidence will disappear when we need it most.

What makes this form of doubt so powerful is that we seldom, if ever, have much control over the diverse factors that make up our working environments, including the people, events and activities that are part of them. In fact, because our confidence is typically circumstantial, we do not even feel we have control over our own feelings of confidence.

Doubt about control is best dealt with through *observed acceptance*, which is about observing things as they are and responding to the best of our ability. Doubt about control is mostly the product of irrational pseudo-thinking when we are on autopilot. It adds no value whatsoever. When we are present, we observe things as they are and can respond accordingly. The one thing we stand the greatest chance of controlling is ourselves. When we are on autopilot, emotionally and mentally hijacked, this is just not going to happen.

### 7. Doubt about Effort

The final form of doubt is the negative thinking about the effort we are making while in the Stretch Zone. This negative thinking relates not so much to whether we initiate action, as to the extent of our effort and the effect thereof. At the heart of this form of doubt is the fear that we are not doing enough to make an acceptable impact. The doubt does not precede action; instead, the doubt arises during the action as the monkey-mind constantly questions our effort and impact, dividing our faculties and undermining our confidence and impact in the process.

What makes this form of doubt so challenging is that those individuals with a predisposition to doubt themselves in this way are typically especially quick off the mark and in the thick of the action. As a result they are often oblivious to the positive impact they are having and question the extent of their effort. As they question themselves, they try even harder, getting caught up in lots of unnecessary and frenetic *doing* – beyond which they struggle to see.

Doubt about effort is best handled through *measured effort*, where a willingness to give things a go and a sound work ethic are not lost, but measured in relation to time and place. *Pause to connect* enables these individuals to stop and observe what is going on. *Connected attention* focuses attention on the performance itself and not on their doubt about whether they are doing enough. With measure and composure, their confidence releases and their impact increases substantially.

## Self-Limiting Doubt – A P.A.C.K.A.G.E. Deal

We need to keep in mind that the above patterns pertain to the content of our doubt, the what we doubt, and that the content is not the key factor. The decisive factor is the act of doubting itself. *That* we doubt is the problem; *what* we doubt is just a detail over which we need not become overly bothered.

Experience has demonstrated to me that each of us usually succumbs to two or three specific forms of doubt. There are, however, no particular rules about this and you simply need to observe them for yourself. Once you know the patterns, spotting the doubts within yourself is not that difficult and you'll most likely have recognised some already.

Let us turn once more to the double-edged sword of knowledge and awareness. Firstly, we need to be aware of the doubt. Secondly, we need to know that 'I am not the doubt'. Seen from the vantage point of the *detached* conscious observer, the inner sage, we need to remember that we are not the doubt: it is just pseudo-thinking in the mind. What we find beyond the doubt is an *abundance of potential, talent and capability*.

> 'What we find beyond the doubt is an abundance of potential, talent and capability.'

As an aide-memoire, the seven forms of doubt create the acronym P.A.C.K.A.G.E., as summarised in the following table.

| Doubt | Fear | Measure |
| --- | --- | --- |
| Pace | Fear of being too slow | Poised Calm |
| Ability | Fear of not being good enough | Curious Exploration |
| Control | Fear of the unexpected | Observed Acceptance |
| Knowledge | Fear of not knowing | Appropriate Balance |
| Acceptance | Fear of being rejected | Genuine Self-Acceptance |
| Goal | Fear of failure | Focused Performance |
| Effort | Fear of not doing enough | Measured Effort |

Once placed under conscious observation, doubt becomes completely powerless and can no longer undermine our confidence and performance potential. The key is to observe it in the Stretch Zone, when it really matters.

**In Summary**

1. To unlearn doubt, we need to observe and recognise those patterns that undermine us.

2. Given our differences, we all doubt ourselves in our own different ways, in different situations.

3. Doubt typically relates to pace, ability, control, knowledge, acceptance, goals and effort.

4. As soon as we observe the doubt within ourselves, we need to remember 'I am not the doubt'.

## 53. Personality and Confidence

I often hear people tell me in coaching conversations that confidence is not really a possibility for them, given the particular mix of their personality. The underlying idea is that confidence is the domain of some personalities, to the exclusion of others.

---
**Key Question:**

To what extent does your personality have an impact on your feelings of confidence?

---

An individual might, for example, cautiously step back to reflect before taking action – thereby creating the impression that she lacks confidence. When she sees others leap forward without hesitation, this only entrenches her ego-identity – 'I am not confident' – even more deeply. In this way, personality can undermine confidence.

From my own experience, I have found no evidence to suggest that confidence is the domain of only certain types of personality to the exclusion of others. People of vastly different personality types can either lack or exude confidence. In fact, people with very different personality types can want to develop confidence. These include those who seem happy to lead boldly from the front, yet who, given the right circumstances, will reveal their doubt. They fear that people will see through them, that their confidence is no more than a veneer masking insecurities, just like the rest of us often feel.

The notion that confidence is limited to certain personality types is a misconception, a myth that seems to be pretty widespread today. I have found that people who doubt their own capacity for confidence by virtue of their personality are often quite surprised to hear that seemingly confident people also seek to develop confidence. The more we indulge in this assumption, the greater is its power to undermine.

So what is the nature of the relationship between personality and confidence? What effect does personality really have on confidence? And in what ways might confidence be different for different personality types?

## Justified Inadequacy

The assumption that personality can preclude confidence is a coping mechanism we use to justify our own sense of inadequacy. When we justify our perceived inadequacy we inadvertently give ourselves an excuse to avoid the Stretch Zone – because 'I just don't have it'. This justification is an *avoidance strategy* whereby we give ourselves permission to hold back and withdraw into our *comfort zone*.

Never allow yourself to justify a perceived inadequacy. Both fight and flight are *habitual coping mechanisms* that are entrenched within our *acquired nature*. That is not who you are. That is the 'little you', the fictitious ego-identity in the form of the inner idiot. It'll never allow you to discover your potentiality.

## Personal Styles and Preferences

Everyday experience suggests that while we are all different, we tend to behave in similar ways. Some people make decisions quickly, others take more time. Some are organised, others less so. While some are more concerned with ensuring everyone works harmoniously together, others are more interested in delivering results. In these ways and more, people are different and we can view personality style as a collection of behaviour patterns according to which individuals are *more like this* and *less like that*.

Personality *styles* create a corresponding *preference* in behaviour, giving us a greater inclination towards one type of behaviour than to another. For example, results-driven people tend to behave in ways that are conducive towards results delivery. People-focused individuals behave in a way that reflects their concern for the wellbeing of people over and above results. While structured people tend to adopt a step-by-step approach to tasks, unstructured people tend to take a more haphazard approach. Whatever your style, you are likely to have a *particular behavioural preference* which matches that style and which is likely to *feel familiar* and comfortable.

> 'Whatever your style, you are likely to have a particular behavioural preference that matches that style and which is likely to feel familiar and comfortable.'

Emerging out of your style and corresponding preferences is a *predisposition* towards a pattern of behaviour. Because your mode of preferred behaviour is comfortable for you – a *comfort zone* – you will tend to repeat it over and over again, entrenching it within your *acquired nature*. In effect, we all become predisposed to behave in a particular way and to deviate from this behaviour is not very easy for us. Most of this takes place when we are operating on autopilot.

While the differences between personality types are pretty much common sense, psychologists have formalised them into a range of psychometric tools which compare and contrast personalities in relation to a particular series of contrasting styles. For example, many psychometric self-assessments compare and contrast personality in relation to *introversion* and *extroversion*. These contrasting styles are generalisations and by no means complete reflections of individual personalities. A human being is far too unique to be defined in the either/or terms of a psychometric self-assessment. To take the results of a psychometric test as fact, as absolute truth or a complete picture would be like doing surgery with a hacksaw. However, while they have their shortcomings, these tests can provide a handy way of understanding personality.

If considering your own personality in relation to a psychometric test, it is important to be aware that the contrasting dimensions of personality are not about 'good' or 'bad', 'better' or 'worse'. They are about *difference* and about being aware of these differences within yourself and others. Neither introversion nor extroversion is better than the other. They are simply different. What is important is your awareness of your preferences and predispositions and the effect these have on yourself, on others and on your performance potential.

People who are unfamiliar with the notion of personality differences tend to think that everyone else has similar preferences to themselves. It is only when given the opportunity to consider personality differences that it dawns on these individuals that other human beings are different to them and that their preference is not necessarily the same as everyone else's. Psychologists make a lot of money out of this simple mistake. While this might sound ridiculous, when taking groups through a psychometric self-assessment I have found that many people experience a real light-bulb moment. That was certainly my own experience first time round.

The more we are aware of our personal styles and preferences, the more we are able to *flex* our style to *match* those of others. In so doing, we are better able to engage positively with people of different preferences. When flexing your own style, it is helpful to be aware of the extent to which you have a particular predisposition. To better understand this predisposition, psychometric self-assessments usually measure preferences on a bar chart which reflects the extent to which a particular preference is mild, moderate, strong or extreme. While a mild or moderate preference is relatively easy to flex and not so obvious to others, a strong or extreme preference becomes increasingly more difficult to flex and tends to clash a lot more with the opposite preference. In this way, our personality is coloured by our preferences and the extent to which we are predisposed in certain directions (see Figure 32).

Psychometric Bar Chart

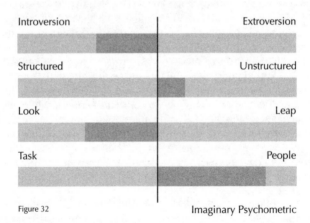

Figure 32        Imaginary Psychometric

## A Word of Caution

Psychometric self-assessments really should come with a health warning. Any attempt to categorise a human being into a particular *pigeon hole* is a gross oversimplification of human potential. At best, a psychometric self-assessment is a snap shot of our personality and not the personality as a whole. In as much as a single photo might say very little about someone's life, a psychometric test actually says very little about the person. To come to any conclusions based on the psychometric self-assessment is inadvisable, yet many do.

Whenever I use a psychometric test, I always draw a picture of a bucket on a flipchart and ask people what is inside. After some guesses from the group, I say that just as we sometimes say we need to take something with a pinch of salt, so we need to take the psychometric test with a bucket of salt. It simply is not who we are – it is only a *very limited snap shot*, a reflection of the ego-identity and *acquired nature*. A psychometric test will tell you absolutely nothing about consciousness, the detached conscious observer, the inner sage, or your *essential nature*, all of which are by far more potent in transforming your performance potential.

Psychometric self-assessments may even limit us owing to the power of the self-fulfilling prophesy. If you tell a child that he is no good, that is precisely what he is likely to become. Similarly, if we believe 'I am introverted or extroverted', 'structured or unstructured', that is what we will end up with – a limited ego-identity. Using the vantage point of the conscious observer, we can be whatever we choose to be. To be *outstanding* and exceptional, we need to *stand out* from the crowd and come out of the herd mentality of autopilot. When we are consciously present we have conscious choice as to who we are and how we would like to behave.

I have even come across a psychometric self-assessment that sets *confidence* in opposition to *caution*, which implies that caution precludes confidence. Common sense tells us that in some situations being cautious requires confidence, especially when everyone else is leaping in feet first. I cannot overemphasise the fact that confidence is not the exclusive domain of some personality styles to the exclusion of others.

Confidence is *independent of personality* and will simply *manifest differently* depending on our individual preferences. I have found that, as soon as people realise this, their natural confidence releases and they find within themselves the confidence to achieve their performance potential.

> 'Confidence is independent of personality and will simply manifest differently depending on our individual preferences.'

Confidence is the natural state for all human beings regardless of personality; it only looks and sounds different according to who we are. Genuine confidence is about *being confident* in a way that is congruent with your own character and not trying to fake it to be like someone else. If we try to *emulate* others, we will find the facade is neither convincing nor sustainable. Real confidence comes naturally from within ourselves, in a manner that is congruent with our nature, with our individual styles and preferences.

## Contrasting Dimensions in Styles and Preferences

While there are many psychometric tests available today, some good and some dodgy, they essentially cover a similar range of personality traits and dimensions. Besides these seemingly scientific tools are other informal, less scientific tools such as those which group personalities in one of four categories, for example. These generally include the action-orientated doer, the reflective thinker, the empathetic friend and the outgoing entertainer. Because psychometrics are as inexact as they are, these informal Cosmopolitan-like self-assessments are generally just as good in practice as their more scientific counterparts, providing a common language with which to understand personality differences and flex our own behaviours accordingly.

The next section outlines some basic ways to contrast personalities, which we'll build on over the next two chapters.

### 1. Introversion vs. Extroversion

Introversion and extroversion are opposite dimensions of personality which are often confused with the extent to which an individual is sociable or unsociable. However, these two dimensions are actually about how we absorb energy. Tired after a busy day, extroverts prefer to re-charge their batteries by being with other people, whereas introverts prefer to recharge with some time out for themselves. Just as an extrovert would find recharging by taking some quiet time to be their worst nightmare, so introverts, when tired, are likely to find engaging with lots of people to be their worst case scenario. It is all about personal choice and preference.

A key characteristic of introverts is that they tend to think through their thoughts internally and then vocalise the conclusion. Extroverts, in contrast, vocalise their thoughts and the conclusion. So with the extrovert we get to witness the whole process and with the introvert we get the conclusion only. It does not take much imagination to see how these different styles often clash, with an extrovert wishing the introvert would say something and the introvert wishing the extrovert would make a point.

### 2. Structured vs. Unstructured

A predisposition for structure implies a preference to approach tasks methodically, beginning at the beginning and working through step-by-step. People with a preference for less or no structure are quite happy to approach a task in a haphazard manner, beginning with whatever feels right and jumping from this to that. For example, when setting up a new DVD player, an unstructured person is more likely to try to do it by themselves, only looking at the manual now and again. A structured person is more likely to work through the instructions in a step-by-step manner.

It is easy to see how the contrasting styles might clash, with unstructured people becoming frustrated with their structured friends, who they think cramp their style. Equally, unstructured people are likely to frustrate the structured among us by flitting from this to that.

### 3. Look vs. Leap

'Look vs. leap' refers to how we approach new situations or problems: some people like to look before they leap, whereas others like to leap straight in, feet first. People who like to look before they leap have a preference to reflect before they act, displaying composed patience and taking a carefully considered approach.

When they feel they have some clarity on the way forward, they engage in action. In contrast, people who like to leap straight into action are those individuals who want to get on with things, driven by a sense of urgency and the desire to get things moving.

The clash is again very obvious. The 'leapers' are likely to be impatient with the reflective 'lookers'. The lookers are likely to feel pressured by the leapers. While the leapers are likely to question whether the lookers will actually get anything done, the lookers are likely to question whether the leapers will get the right thing done well.

### 4. Task vs. People

Task-focused people tend to be highly results orientated and do all they can to make sure the results are delivered as the highest priority. Their outlook is that the end will justify the means and this gives them licence to come across as directive, decisive and pushy. People-focused individuals put other people and relationships first, over and above results delivery. They tend to exercise patience, making sure everyone is involved, has their say and that everyone is happy.

Clearly the two styles can rub each other up the wrong way. Task-focused people become frustrated by what they view to be unnecessary diversions which impede delivery. People-focused individuals become frustrated by their task-orientated peers' perceived blatant disregard for the humanity of those who are actually going to deliver the results.

None of the contrasting styles can claim superiority over its contrasting partner. In fact, philosophers would suggest that the very existence of each style is defined only by the existence of its counterpart. We only have wet because we have dry, high because we have low and left because we have right, for example. Without the reference point that each provides the other, none of the styles would actually be grounded in anything. With this in mind, the contrasting styles are clearly *not about being better than*, only *different to*.

However, as a result of our stereotypical prejudices, we tend to associate confidence with some personality dimensions to the exclusion of others. So what does this actually look like in practice?

---

**In Summary**

1.  Confidence is NOT the domain of certain personalities to the exclusion of others.

2.  Confidence is independent of personality; it only looks and sounds different according to who we are.

3.  The belief that confidence is limited by personality is used to justify our own feelings of inadequacy.

4.  Personality consists of different dimensions, styles and behavioural preferences.

5.  No behavioural preference is better than any other; it is only different.

---

## 54. Confidence – A Conditioned Stereotype

It has become apparent to me over the years that our potential is often undermined by our stereotypical view of confidence – of what we think it looks and sounds like. Based on our misconceived paradigm, we associate confidence with some personality dimensions to the exclusion of others.

---

**Key Question:**

Referring once more to the personality dimensions we discussed in the last chapter, how might you be tempted to describe confidence as a conditioned stereotype?

---

Given the competitive, results-driven world we've created for ourselves, it is not surprising that many of us view confidence as a trait of aggressive and pushy stereotypes. Whether it is aggressiveness at the office, on the sports field, at the shopping mall, or with friends and family, we so often confuse confidence with a character quirk of that pushy so-and-so who does everything to be top dog.

However, if we scratch below the surface a very different picture emerges. Pushy people have learnt that an aggressive approach often elicits fear in others, enabling them to have the upper hand. By intimidating others, they also hope that their own fear and doubt will remain hidden and, in keeping this hidden, that others will see them as capable and confident.

In the real world, the pushy stereotype is nothing other than a circumstantially dependent facade of *pseudo-confidence* and one that can only fool some of the people some of the time. Sooner or later, the cracks begin to show and the pushy person goes from top dog to mutt in a blink of an eye.

**Example: An Aggressive Leader**

When I was facilitating a senior leadership programme some years ago, it was fascinating to observe how a senior but aggressive leader quickly lost his position of influence and credibility as people saw through his pushy facade. His projection of *pseudo-confidence* simply could not match the emerging, more genuine confidence in those around him. It was so sad to hear him open up in one-to-one coaching about his underlying fears and anxieties, but as soon as he was back in the group he immediately reverted back to his conditioned facade, thereby inadvertently undermining his impact and credibility.

As mentioned previously, the trouble with being top dog is that sooner or later someone will test your metal and the game will be up.

### Conditioned Stereotype and Contrasting Styles

As a result of widely-held stereotypical views, we tend to associate confidence with certain personality dimensions rather than their corresponding traits. The effect is that confidence becomes a greater possibility with some traits to the exclusion of others. So what would this look like with each of the dimensions outlined previously?

### 1. Introversion vs. Extroversion

We are typically conditioned to associate confidence more readily with *extroverted* people – those who are outspoken, thinking their thoughts aloud. In contrast, *introverted* people, who process their thoughts internally, come across as quietly cautious.

### 2. Structured vs. Unstructured

Similarly, *structured* people are typically seen as less confident as they cautiously work things out step by step; whereas *unstructured* people often appear bold and fearless, as they jump into situations with what might seem like carefree abandon.

### 3. Look vs. Leap

Equally, people who like to *look* before they leap, preferring to consider and reflect before acting, tend to be seen as cautious and hesitant, compared to those who prefer to *leap* straight in, feet first.

### 4. Task vs. People

Lastly, *people-focused* individuals can come across as cautious in their concern for others. However, their *task-focused* counterparts are often seen as bold and confident as they push through their intentions without much concern for the effect of these on others.

Keeping these preconceived stereotypes in mind and our responses to them, there is little wonder that we frequently feel our own personality mix precludes confidence. That said, it is interesting to note that I frequently come across people who invert the stereotypes and associate confidence with the opposite quality of those we have just considered above. Regardless of which way it goes, however, we are all inclined to use our stereotypical views as a means to justify our own perceived inadequacy, thereby undermining our confidence.

**In Summary**

1. Our conditioned idea of confidence is often that of the aggressive, pushy stereotype.

2. The pushy stereotype is a circumstantially dependent facade of *pseudo-confidence*.

3. Confidence is often associated with task-focused extroverts who leap into action.

4. Preferences for introversion, for working with people, structure and reflection do not preclude confidence.

## 55. Confidence for ALL without Exception

Confidence is, as we have seen, by no means the exclusive domain of only certain personality types to the exclusion of others. It is an imminent reality for anyone, anywhere, anytime, regardless of style and preference. In fact, confidence has nothing to do with what we would ordinarily call 'personality': our personality only colours the way that our confidence looks and sounds.

> **Key Question:**
>
> What is it about confidence, do you think, that makes it independent of personality?

Confidence is independent of personality for the very reason that what we ordinarily refer to as personality is nothing other than our *acquired nature*. Confidence has nothing to do with our *acquired nature*. Confidence is a state, part of our *essential nature*. It is not something we acquire along the way. While doubt might be a learnt behaviour, confidence is our natural state. Even in the Stretch Zone.

In our everyday lives, we might refer to someone as having a confident personality. Yet, when we take another look, it is not very difficult to recognise that we can be confident in many different ways. Someone might be seen as confident, charismatic, outgoing and outspoken. However, someone else might be seen as confident, quiet and focused, with real stillness and presence.

### Confidence across Styles and Preferences

As mentioned previously, those of us who appear to exude confidence are frequently only too aware that all is not necessarily as it might seem on the surface. Similarly, those of us who seem to lack confidence are by no means a lost cause. Outspoken, task-focused, results-driven extroverts are likely to be seen as *more confident*. Thoughtful, reflective, people-focused introverts are frequently seen as *less confident*. However, things are not always as they might seem.

In the context of our results-driven, competitive world, where taking action and delivering results are regarded as ideals, people who like to look before they leap often see themselves as less adequate than those who are quicker to action. In training, people will frequently skew their answers in psychometric testing so that they come across as action-orientated doers – when clearly they are not. This is just an ego thing and it quickly becomes apparent. To assume that a preference to reflect before action is a limitation is nonsense, and the effect of trying to mimic this preference is to elicit doubt and undermine confidence.

I have found that as soon as people become more aware of their styles and preferences – and realise that no preference is better than any other, they *give themselves permission* to follow their preferences, which makes a world of difference. When, for example, people give themselves the space to look before they leap, they no longer doubt themselves when doing so and their confidence follows accordingly. The critical factor is to recognise that the doubt associated with the clash between our *perceived pressure to react quickly* and our *preference to reflect* is completely irrational. In this way we can give ourselves permission to be reflective, introverted, structured and people-focused – and to be fearless and confident in the process.

---

**Example: Pausing Before Action**

Pausing before action can be the most intelligent and courageous thing to do in certain circumstances. Yet reflective introverts often feel a tremendous pressure to react quickly. The perceived pressure to react quickly is a conditioned habitual behaviour which thrives when we are on autopilot. It is an irrational habit. As soon as we give ourselves conscious permission to pause, our doubt will diminish – enabling us to stand out from the crowd and make a substantial impact.

---

When reflective introverts give themselves conscious permission to act in ways that are congruent with their nature, their impact escalates immediately. Reflective introverts often display a quiet composure, an underlying stillness and presence. When they give themselves permission to reflect their true selves, and their composure comes across in their speech and actions, the results can be highly influential and next to impossible to ignore.

The quality and impact of any action is a direct reflection of the inner state within which that action began. Given their potential for stillness and presence, when reflective introverts give themselves permission to pause before action, the quality and impact of that action directly reflects their state within. The pause preceding action enables reflective introverts to come out of autopilot and act from conscious presence – when they are good and ready. The inner and outer feedback loops strengthen their confidence even further.

> 'The quality and impact of any action is a direct reflection of the inner state within which that action began.'

## The Action-Orientated Doers

This is not to dismiss the more extroverted, action-orientated doers. Their preferences are as much a conditioned habit as their more introverted cousin's predisposition for reflection. Their tendency to leap into action is usually a knee-jerk reaction that is no guarantee of success. What they quickly discover is that their conditioned predisposition for action often creates an increased pressure that, in spite of attempts to mask it, can sometimes limit their impact substantially.

When they give themselves permission to pause, even briefly, before they leap into action, they are usually in a far stronger position to make a positive impact than when they leap straight in out of conditioned habit. A pause preceding action enables the action-orientated doers to come out of autopilot and all the habitual conditioning that accompanies it. So, without losing their drive towards action and results, they are better placed to deliver efficiently and effectively.

As we have seen, the quality and impact of any action remains a direct reflection of the inner state within which that action began. If the action arose out of conditioned habit rooted in autopilot, the quality and impact of that action will reflect this. If the action arises out of conscious presence, the quality and impact will reflect this too. Whether we are an action-orientated doer or a people-orientated reflector, a *pause to connect* transforms our inner state and performance potential. If you practise this, it will set you apart; it will give you the means to be exceptional and the results you seek will follow, inevitably.

**In Summary**

1.  Confidence is independent of personality, which relates to our *acquired nature*.

2.  Confidence is a state, part of our *essential nature*.

3.  Confidence is an imminent potential for ALL; it only looks and sounds different depending on our personality and experience.

4.  Genuine confidence is congruent with our different personal styles and preferences.

5.  The quality of any action is a direct reflection of the inner state within which that action began.

6.  When reflectors and doers pause before action, their impact increases substantially.

## Part Ten
# A Fourth Principle

## 56. Trust Yourself, Be Yourself, Enjoy Yourself

The three primary principles of confidence – the absence of doubt, confidence as our natural state and a state of detached interest – bring us to a fourth principle: *confidence as a state of readiness*. This fourth principle has come up time and again in a coaching and facilitation context.

---

**Key Question:**

Given the three principles, what in your view is the most obvious next step?

---

While the three primary principles create the conditions within which confidence is inevitable, what remains is for each of us simply to step out of our comfort zone and engage in the Stretch Zone. Until we step out of it and engage, we cannot hope to make any kind of impact. The fourth principle is therefore about *stepping up* to meet adversity. The moment we do this, we cross an imaginary line from uncertainty to certainty, from indecision to decision, from doubt to confidence. Transitioning through that crossroads is to see the world and to approach any given situation from a distinctly different point of view, a very different paradigm.

---

'Until we step out of our comfort zones and engage, we cannot hope to make any kind of impact.'

---

### A State of Readiness

The definition of confidence as a state of readiness implies that we are ready to step up and take action. Taking action means a whole lot of different things and, depending on the situation, sometimes inaction can be the best action. Less is so often more. Having brought our *inner performance* to that heightened state of readiness, all that remains is for us to engage through our *outer performance*.

Confidence as a state of readiness implies *trust* in ourselves and in our capacity to perform to our potential. With trust, we let go and engage. This trust is not about piling on the pressure to achieve a particular outcome, but to do our best in the circumstances. When we resolve to do our best we give ourselves *permission* to step up, engage and let things unfold as they may. We have absolutely no idea how things will turn out. The outcome is a *potential future reality* that is yet to become an *actual present reality*.

The fourth principle also implies making the *decision* to enter the Stretch Zone. With indecision and procrastination, doubt and inadequacy thrive. As soon as we make a decision to engage, our faculties align themselves to the effort and our potential becomes a certainty. When we dither, our faculties vacillate with indecision, undermining our potential.

Until the point at which we make a *conscious decision* to step up and engage, our thoughts, speech and actions are likely to be determined by the *unconscious decision* to hold back and withdraw into our comfort zones. When faced with adversity, a decision is made and it is either an unconscious conditioned decision to hesitate or a conscious decision to let go and engage.

When we make a decision, trust, step up and engage, not only do our inner faculties align themselves to the effort, *opportunities* will also arise to meet us along the way – opportunities that we are unlikely to have been aware of previously. With indecision we have one point of view, with decision we have an entirely different point of view, and opportunities that support our decision will present themselves. When we make a decision to engage, the forces of the universe align themselves to meet and support our decision. What opportunities come our way will only be known once we have stepped up.

As we step up we find that we have something constructive to focus on. As long as we procrastinate, our attention jumps from one doubt to another as we mindlessly imagine what might happen. When we engage, our faculties focus, aligning themselves to the effort. So while the three primary principles create the conditions within which confidence is inevitable, the fourth principle is about stepping up from within that heightened state of readiness.

## Transitioning the Crossroads

This transition at the crossroads between our comfort zones and the Stretch Zone appears again and again in a coaching and facilitation context. There are five important things to keep in mind:

### 1. Trust Yourself

So often when coaching, the conversation will get to a point where I find myself saying, 'Trust yourself.' What usually follows is a pause, a moment of reflection. The crux of the matter is that when it matters most, we just don't trust ourselves. We'd rather trust anybody else than ourselves. Above all else, we need to remember to trust ourselves.

### 2. Remember Yourself

The Oracle of Delphi enjoins mankind to 'know thyself'. We are the only common denominator in every waking moment of our lives. Yet mostly we only know what we are not – the transitory ego-identity. So, above all else, we need to remember ourselves, and to view ourselves with the limitless potentiality of the conscious observer. When we remember ourselves, trusting ourselves is easy.

### 3. Accept Yourself

Very often, we simply do not genuinely accept ourselves for who and what we are. When we are not accepting ourselves we are rejecting ourselves, with self-criticism undermining our every intention. Genuine confidence is about self-acceptance, about accepting ourselves for who and what we are in that particular moment.

### 4. Be Yourself

The best thing you can do is to be yourself. We cannot be anyone else, yet we so often spend so much time and energy trying to be like someone else. To be yourself is to remember, trust and accept yourself. To be yourself is to be true to yourself, to be authentic and congruent. In Shakespeare's *Hamlet*, the character of Polonius suggests: 'This above all: to thine own self be true, And it must follow, as night the day, Thou canst not then be false to any man.'

> 'This above all: to thine own self be true, And it must follow as night the day, Thou canst not then be false to any man.'
>
> William Shakespeare

### 5. Enjoy Yourself

The saying goes: 'life is too short.' So we might as well enjoy each moment for what it is. Facing adversity is no different: adversity tests our limits and challenges our capabilities. Life without adversity would be boring, not worth living. It is only when we stretch ourselves that we really begin to know and enjoy ourselves. So give your *inner child* permission, have fun and enjoy those challenging moments with carefree abandon.

The three primary principles create the conditions within which confidence is inevitable, a heightened state of readiness. The next step is to trust yourself and step out of your comfort zone into the Stretch Zone – and enjoy the moment. The great beauty is that we never know what might happen until we actually *know*.

> 'The great beauty is that we never know what might happen until we actually know.'

**In Summary**

1. Until we step up and engage we cannot hope to make any kind of impact.

2. Confidence as a state of readiness is about *stepping up* and crossing an imaginary line.

3. *Stepping up* is about trusting ourselves.

4. *Stepping up* replaces an unconscious conditioned decision with a conscious decision.

5. As soon as we make that conscious decision, opportunities begin to present themselves along the way.

## 57. Unexpected Opportunities

Stepping across the threshold from our comfort zone into the Stretch Zone is not always that easy. The transition entails moving from what is safe and secure into the unknown. Not only does it feel uncomfortable, it can also feel quite lonely. The saying is 'it's lonely at the top' – and that is how we so often feel when stepping into the Stretch Zone.

---

**Key Question:**

When stepping into the Stretch Zone, what have you often discovered along the way?

---

Leaving our comfort zone and stepping across the threshold into the Stretch Zone might not seem that easy and it might even feel uncomfortable. On the other hand, it is actually quite easy to do. Moreover, once we have made the transition and we turn around and look back, we will find that the obstacles we thought were there are not actually there – they were only imagined. More often than not, the greatest impediment to making that transition is yourself. All you need to do is to step forward and begin at the beginning.

To avoid stepping across that threshold is to perpetuate the repetitive conditioning of fear and doubt that has more likely than not plagued your life for a long time. It is to retreat further within your comfort zone, swallowing the bitter pill of anxiety and regret, of self-recrimination and denial, and continuing to suppress what you have most likely suppressed for years. American entrepreneur Seth Godin puts it nicely, saying: 'Anxiety is nothing... but repeatedly re-experiencing failure in advance. What a waste.' The only alternative is to step up with conscious intention.

---

'Anxiety is nothing... but repeatedly re-experiencing failure in advance. What a waste.'

Seth Godin

---

**Encouraging the Heart**

So why should we take heart and step into the Stretch Zone? This chapter outlines some truths about why we should cross that imaginary threshold.

### 1. Conscious Presence

We are, first and foremost, conscious beings with a mental, emotional and physical existence. When we come out of autopilot, our conscious presence expands and is brought to bear on the present moment. With the power of our consciousness, we can face whatever comes our way, without exception. With consciousness we find, within us, the essential creative force upon which everything else is dependent. So fear nothing and trust in your conscious presence to enable you to deal with things as they arise.

### 2. Our Natural State

When we come out of an emotionally or mentally hijacked state, our *acquired nature*, with all its fears and doubts, gives way to our *essential nature*. As a force, nothing on earth is more powerful than Mother Nature. To act against our nature is not very easy. Our essential nature is to be happy, spontaneous, fearless, present, creative, perceptive and confident. So fear nothing and trust in the power of your essential nature to enable you to deal with things as they arise.

### 3. Faculties Aligned

When we come into the present, all our faculties of mind, heart, reason, nature, senses, perception and attention come into their natural alignment. When our powers are combined and aligned, they act on whatever is in front of us with remarkable force. So fear nothing and trust in the power of your faculties to enable you to deal with things as they arise.

### 4. Begin at the Beginning

When faced with adversity the best place to start is at the beginning. But where is the beginning? The beginning is not in the situation itself, in external events out there. The beginning is within yourself, when you come out of autopilot into the present. The quality and impact of any action is directly dependent on the nature of the inner state out of which that action arises. So fear nothing and trust that when you begin at the beginning you'll be able to deal with things as they arise.

### 5. Different Point of View

As we step up, our point of view changes, enabling us to see things quite differently. From our renewed point of view, what we had assumed to be real from within our hijacked state is no longer real. From this different point of view, the situation, problem, other people and even ourselves will all look distinctly different. So fear nothing and trust that when you step up you'll see things differently – and that will enable you to deal with things as they arise.

### 6. Unexpected Opportunities

As we step up into the Stretch Zone opportunities present themselves along the way. When we step up providence steps up to meet us in our moment of need. So fear nothing and trust that opportunities will present themselves, enabling you to deal with things as they arise.

'Until one is committed, there is hesitancy, the chance to draw back. Concerning all acts of initiative (and creation), there is one elementary truth, the ignorance of which kills countless ideas and splendid plans: that the moment one definitely commits oneself, then Providence moves too. All sorts of things occur to help one that would never otherwise have occurred. A whole stream of events issues from the decision, raising in one's favour all manner of unforeseen incidents and meetings and material assistance, which no man could have dreamed would have come his way. Whatever you can do, or dream you can do, begin it. Boldness has genius, power, and magic in it. Begin it now.'

Goethe

### 7. Special Knowledge

When we come out of our hijacked state into the present, the ordinary knowledge that is limited to memory of past conditioning becomes secondary to a very different level of knowledge. With presence comes that special knowledge of the present moment, which only comes within that moment. That special knowledge brings whatever you need to know within that moment. So fear nothing and trust that you'll have the knowledge to be able to deal with things as they arise.

### 8. Step by Step

When we doubt ourselves, what we doubt most is our capacity to take the situation to the next step and then the next. From the point of view of our hijacked state and comfort zone, our capacity to see ahead is severely limited. When we step up with presence, from that refreshed point of view the next step becomes clear to us. So fear nothing and trust that the way forward will become clear and will enable you to deal with things as they arise.

---

**The Man and the Lantern, a Traditional Story**

A man had to make a long journey late at night from his village to the next, a journey of many miles. When he stepped out of his home he found that it was pitch dark outside and his little lantern only shone its light a few feet in front of him. A wise man happened to pass that way and asked him why he was standing outside his front door with a lantern. Having heard the explanation, the wise man reassured the man that he need not worry as with every step forward the light of the lantern will also move forward – and he will always be able to see where he is going.

Anon

---

### 9. Inner Sage

Stepping up is so much easier when we know that we have an experienced soul stepping up alongside us. When we come into the present, the inner idiot, being the coward it is, disappears into the nothingness from which it came. Emerging out of its shadow is our inner sage with all the wisdom, temperance and intention we need to guide us along the way. So fear nothing and trust that you have the wisdom to enable you to deal with things along the way.

### 10. Mind over Matter

If you don't mind, it doesn't matter. When we come into the present all our preferences, fears, doubts, desires and aversions all fade into less significance. They simply become less important and they just don't matter as much. Because we don't mind so much, the rocks and stones – the important things in our lives – find their place within the jar and all the rest – the sand – just doesn't really matter. When free from the battle within, our faculties come to bear on the present. So fear nothing and trust that things will work themselves out one way or another, and that you'll be able to deal with things as they arise.

> 'Nothing can stop the man with the right mental attitude from achieving his goal, nothing on earth can help the man with the wrong attitude.'
>
> Thomas Jefferson

And don't forget that another really good reason why we should take heart and face life's challenges is that *we can*. When we truly realise we can, *we can*. We cannot always choose *what* we face, but we can choose *how* we face it. So fear nothing and trust that you have everything you need to deal with things as they arise.

There are many reasons why we should take heart, fearlessly. Doubt is an impostor and makes us 'small'. When small and self-limiting, we can never expect to transcend our limitations and achieve our potential. It is only when we step out of our smallness and into our greatness that we begin to discover who we really are and what we are really capable of. Stephen Covey is known for a few quotes, but my favourite, which is less well known than many of his others, is: 'The main thing is to keep the main thing, the main thing.' And the main thing is to transform our inner state by being consciously present at the *moment-of-impact*.

> 'The main thing is to keep the main thing, the main thing.'
>
> Stephen Covey

**In Summary**

1. Stepping across the threshold from our comfort zone into the Stretch Zone is not always that easy.

2. Consciousness, the ultimate creative force, is on our side when we are present.

3. *Being confident* is our *essential nature* – and there is nothing more powerful than Nature.

4. When we are present, our faculties align and come to bear on the present moment.

5. Stepping up begins at the beginning and that means coming out of autopilot into the present.

6. As we step up, opportunities will meet us along the way.

7. With the inner sage comes a fountain of wisdom that supports us in the Stretch Zone.

8. With the right attitude you'll realise that you can – and then *you can*.

## 58. Confidence – A New Paradigm of Possibility

Confidence, in our everyday parlance, is plagued by assumptions and misconceptions that only serve to impede our understanding of it. Beyond this is a new paradigm of possibilities, which is immediately and directly available to everyone without exception.

> **Key Question:**
>
> How would you summarise the differences between the old and new paradigm of confidence?

Based on our day-to-day experience of circumstantial confidence, we believe with complete conviction that confidence is something we lack and need to learn and acquire. In our desperation, we do all that we can to superimpose a projection of *pseudo-confidence* over suppressed fear and doubt. The more our confidence is not there when we need it most, the more convinced we become of its absence until it defines who we think we are with depleted resignation.

### Another Possibility

Confidence is not something we can *have*. It is a state, our natural state. The alternative to *having confidence* is *being confident* by releasing a reservoir of confidence from within.

### *1. Confidence is our Natural State*

Fear and doubt are optional, conditioned habits. Confidence is our natural state, our *essential nature*. Coming from within us, confidence is always an inherent possibility.

### *2. Confidence is Available from Within*

Genuine confidence is not about things or events outside ourselves; it arises from within ourselves. Coming from within, it is authentic, congruent, real and sustainable.

### 3. Confidence is a Constant Potential

While doubt is a transient impostor, confidence is our constant companion. Coming from within, confidence is always available and is independent of time and place.

### 4. Confidence is a Limitless Potential

While our world is filled with finite resources, confidence is infinite and limitless. Rather than become diminished through use, confidence actually increases with use.

### 5. Confidence is a Certainty under Certain Conditions

Confidence is solely dependent on our inner state. When the conditions are appropriate, being confident is a certainty. The key is conscious presence, our inner state of being.

### 6. Confidence is Released by Removing the Doubt

The condition within which confidence becomes an absolute certainty is the *absence of doubt*. With the doubt dispersed, we come into conscious presence, abundantly confident.

### 7. Confidence is a State of Detached Interest

Detached interest is an inner state of freedom from the tyranny of our own self-imposed attachments and conditioning – the freedom of *being confident*.

### 8. Confidence is Independent of Action and Result

Confidence is independent of doing or achieving anything. It is beyond action or inaction, achievement or non-achievement. Confidence is simply composed, poised presence.

### 9. Confidence is Independent of Personality

Rooted within our *essential nature*, confidence is indifferent to personality; it only looks and sounds different according to our personality.

### 10. Confidence Releases our Performance Potential

Confidence is neither the performance nor the achievement that arises out of the performance. Confidence is the catalyst for our performance potential.

If you follow the principles within this book, your fear and doubt will begin to give way to a renewed life of certainty – a life of carefree abandon and creative spontaneity.

**In Summary**

1. The old paradigm of confidence is based on the idea of *having confidence* by acquiring what we lack.

2. The alternative is to realise that confidence is our nature – and simply *be confident*.

## 59. Approaching Life's Crossroads

Without exception, within each waking moment we all of us face diverse crossroads in life. These crossroads present us with choices and contexts within which to make those choices. These choices are not optional, yet we are seldom aware of them at the time. One way or another, we always make choices in the face of our crossroads – each and every moment.

> **Key Question:**
>
> What choices do you face at the crossroads in your life?

### Confidence – A Contemporary Context

The modern world within which we live is the stage upon which we need to express our qualities, talents and aspirations, our purpose, individuality and humanity in whatever way we can. This contemporary stage brings with it considerable comforts which make modern life much easier than it has been for many in the distant past. Yet with *convenience* comes *adversity* as part of the package – adversity that creeps into our lives in many different guises.

The modern globe feels like it's shrunk; the pace of life has increased; change is relentless and the demands and expectations we face each day have gone through the roof. In spite of increased technologies, our capacity to connect with what lies beyond the mundane, beyond the sand in the jar of life, is that much more elusive and so many of us have become that bit more isolated in our society, communities and relationships.

Demands on the work front have increased. Competition for work, resources and opportunities has only added more pressure. Even our time out to relax seems to be under increased pressure, with this precious time frequently being diarised into a particular slot during the summer. In short, while the modern world brings many creature-comforts, it also presents us with many pressures and demands which we have little choice but to face.

The effect of the pushes and pulls of our modern world are not so difficult to see. All manner of individual and social problems, which were previously unheard of, have become common place. It is not surprising that confidence has become such a prevalent issue of our times.

## Confidence – A Contemporary Issue

The confidence that has become such an issue in our modern world is the confidence we have in ourselves, self-confidence. The word 'confidence' comes from the Latin word *confidere*, which means 'to trust, to have faith in an object, situation or person'. In our contemporary world, the person we seem to have the most difficulty trusting is ourselves. While in the past confidence seems to have been about whether or not we held someone else in confidence, today it is mostly about self-confidence and whether we hold ourselves in trust and confidence.

Those who master self-confidence, who exude calm composure and presence, stand out from the crowd. To be confident is to be ahead of the crowd, to have an edge in whatever way we wish to express our qualities, talents and aspirations, our purpose, individuality and humanity.

## Facing the Crossroads

In these challenging times we each face a *crossroads,* a *choice* as to how we choose to live our lives. Within the context of our hurry-up world, this life-choice is about the extent to which we choose a life that is easy, safe, comfortable and predictable; or the extent to which we choose a life that is audacious, bold, courageous and adventurous, a life of purpose and meaning. This life-choice is not optional, it is a given that we each face each and every day, including today.

When consumed with *fear and doubt*, what follows is a small and petty life that always falls short of our potential. With *courage and confidence* we are able to give our best. As we give our best we are able to express our humanity and individuality, our qualities and talents – and to live life to the full. When we give of our best, no matter what we achieve we experience a deep sense of satisfaction, an irreplaceable feeling of happiness and fulfilment – that feeling of vitality and life bursting from within.

## Choice behind the Choice

When we face life's crossroads, our choice is more often than not made for us. Not by anybody else, but by the conditioned habit of the inner idiot. Within our emotionally and mentally hijacked state on autopilot, we are not even aware that we have a choice. The result is a small and petty life, a limited life within which we seldom even glimpse our potentiality.

How often do we stop to consider questions such as: 'what does my life say about me?' 'What does my day-to-day endeavour say about my life?' 'What kind of life would I like to live?' 'What kind of life am I living?' Or, 'what kind of person would I like to be?' In our demanding world we are so busy charging around, doing this and that, taking care of the sand, strutting our hour upon the stage of life, that we tend not to pause and discriminate between what is meaningless and what is meaningful. At the crossroads, we need to make a choice between a life that is defined by *fear and doubt* and a life that is defined by *courage and confidence*.

> 'At the crossroads, we need to make a choice between a life that is defined by fear and doubt and a life that is defined by courage and confidence.'

Shakespeare captures the potential for a petty and fearful life in *Macbeth*:

> Tomorrow, and tomorrow, and tomorrow,
> Creeps in this petty pace from day to day,
> To the last syllable of recorded time;
> And all our yesterdays have lighted fools the way to
> dusty death.
> Out, out, brief candle!
> Life's but a walking shadow, a poor player,
> That struts and frets his hour upon the stage,
> And then is heard no more; it is a tale
> Told by an idiot, full of sound and fury,
> Signifying nothing.

(*Macbeth*, Act Five, scene 5, 19–28)

What is the tale your life speaks of? Is the tale a story of a life lived in fear and doubt, apprehension and caution, an hour upon the stage of life that never truly discovers the potential that is bursting just below the surface of your limited self-conception? To succumb to fear and doubt, putting off until tomorrow and tomorrow and tomorrow is to remain forever within the safe confines of your comfort zone, to miss the very magic that life offers – the magic and adventure that you knew and embraced so freely as a child.

The alternative is a life that is lived to the full, expressing your qualities and talents, pursuing your aspirations in whatever way you wish. At the heart of all this is the confidence within which you meet life, including its comforts and opportunities as well as its challenges and adversities. While we cannot always choose what we face, we can choose how we face it. How we meet the opportunities and challenges life presents us defines who we are; it becomes our tale, our life's story, our hour upon the stage.

> 'While we cannot always choose what we face, we can choose how we face it.'

At the crossroads, the *choice behind the choice* is a choice about who you are. Are you the inner idiot who struts his hour upon the stage, full of sound and fury but actually signifying nothing? Or are you the inner sage, the conscious observer within you, who lives life with enthusiasm, commitment, courage, tenacity, wisdom, compassion, daring, carefree abandon and laughter?

To believe that, when in the face of adversity, we can quickly change our state to one of calm and confidence, is wishful thinking. Our capacity to meet adversity with presence and confidence is directly dependent upon the extent to which we have practised presence and confidence in each moment leading up to the present moment. That is the choice behind the choice.

To embrace and practise the principles and practices presented within *The Stretch Zone* is to embrace the way of self-mastery. To be master of yourself is to master the common denominator within every situation throughout your life – and that is yourself. The Greek sage Epictetus said: 'No man is free who is not master of himself.' Self-mastery begins with mastering our fears and doubts, enabling us to deal with things as they arise. Self-mastery is about meeting life's crossroads from the vantage point of conscious presence.

> 'No man is free who is not master of himself.'
>
> Epictetus

The steadfast and resolute application of the principles and practices presented in these pages will enable much progress in the way of self-mastery. With mastery over yourself, mastery of your abilities and the situations you face becomes an increased probability. You are free to choose a petty life of fear and doubt, or you can choose the courage and confidence that will enable you to become master of yourself. If the latter, you will discover how to express your qualities, talents and aspirations, your purpose, individuality and humanity to the full – with confidence.

**In Summary**

1. Within each waking moment we each face a choice, a crossroads in life.

2. So often the choice is made for us, through our own conditioning, fear and doubt.

3. To choose fear and doubt is to live a small and petty life, squandering your potential.

4. With conscious presence, we can choose life – a bold and audacious life, a life worth living.

5. The *choice behind the choice* is to choose conscious presence over a life on autopilot.

# Case Study

**Confidence and a Driving Phobia**

My coaching with Bev began in February 2008, following her request for help with a problem that had been having a substantial impact on her life for the better part of twenty-seven years. Bev had a driving phobia and even the mere thought of driving would leave her overwhelmed with anxiety. She really wanted to drive – but even the prestigious BMW in her garage was not enough to get her going.

Having previously had the pleasure of working with Bev within a leadership development context, I set up some additional coaching with her to enable her to enjoy driving, anywhere, anytime, with confidence.

**The Nature of a Phobia**

My first step was to make sure I really understood the nature of a phobia, although I had some personal experience from which to draw. Many years ago, when I was a student at the University of Cape Town, I was walking across a small pedestrian bridge when I felt an unexpected anxiety which made me grab hold of the handrail. I had never had a problem with heights before and I put this down to good common sense about standing too close to a potentially large drop.

To this day, whenever I stand too close to a large drop fear arises, which, in my view, is quite rational. However, in some situations such as standing next to a window in a high-rise building, the anxiety that arises in spite of the substantial piece of glass between me and the drop does not strike me as rational. I have, however, never taken this fear of heights very seriously and, as it has little bearing on my life, it has not been much of a problem.

Another experience from which I could draw came from my wife, Sheelagh, who, in spite of growing up in Zimbabwe and Namibia, somehow developed a fear of snakes. Some years ago, when on holiday in Zimbabwe, we had a bit of a tiff (as couples do) and she stormed off into the bush to get away from the half-wit she had married. Seconds later, I heard a piercing scream as Sheelagh came running past me, shouting something about snakes. It was remarkable to observe intelligence displaced by panic within a fraction of a second. Unfortunately, my unintelligent comment did not do much to alleviate the situation.

So, faced with Bev's situation now, I started asking some questions: 'What is a phobia?' 'How do they work?' 'Why do we react in some situations but not in others?' 'Where do phobias come from?' 'Who has the phobia?' 'When it is not around, where does it go?' 'When it is around, where does it come from?' 'What makes a phobia so incapacitating?' 'How can we transcend a phobia?'

A phobia is an irrational fear, a distinct feeling of being out of control, which causes a heightened state of anxiety, dread and panic. In the case of a driving phobia, the phobia has nothing to do with the ability to drive and everything to do with our mental and emotional state when driving. At the heart of a phobia is a complete loss of confidence within the circumstances of the phobia.

Central to understanding a phobia is the intensity of the mental and emotional reaction to the threatening situation. The phobic experience is one of heightened anxiety, a feeling of being overwhelmed and in the grip of something over which the individual believes he has no control. The intensity of the mental and emotional hijacking is traumatic and debilitating, and is accompanied by an apparent loss of rational thought and behaviour.

Given the state within, a phobia is characterised by avoidance behaviours or coping strategies by means of which people hope to deal with the distressing situation. The avoidance behaviours are driven by a burning desire to avoid the threatening situation at any cost, which can limit freedom and quality of life.

### Session One

The first session provided an opportunity to explore Bev's experience. Two things became apparent. Firstly, identifying the past events that may have triggered the phobia was simply not that relevant and unlikely to make the situation go away. While the past has passed, a phobia is perpetuated from within as we create and re-create it ourselves. Naturally, if the cause is still present then something needs to be done about it. Talking about past causes is, at best, cathartic. The real work, however, is in the present.

Secondly, Bev's lack of confidence to drive was accompanied by a broader pattern of anxiety in other situations in her life. Without disclosing these in detail, Bev had acquired a pattern of conditioned self-doubt, which undermined her confidence in specific situations.

When exploring her experience, three distinct phobic patterns became apparent. When faced with having to turn right across an intersection, drive around a traffic island and when someone was driving behind her, Bev would become hijacked by intense self-doubt, a feeling of being completely out of control. And she was certain this had nothing to do with her ability to drive.

Bev had previously sought help by way of cognitive-behavioural therapy, hypnotherapy and psychotherapy – and none of these approaches helped, with some actually exacerbating the situation. Our first session closed with Bev being offered the practice in *conscious awareness*, and making a commitment to practise twice daily.

### Session Two

A week later, our second session began with Bev's experiences of *the practice of conscious awareness*. While practising regularly, she found it more difficult than expected, with her attention being continually distracted from the present moment by random thoughts. Bev was able to recognise that she in no way consciously chose to have these thoughts; they arose unintentionally. This was a positive sign that the practice was going well. To help, we explored the story of the monkey-mind, which became a key part of our conversation going forward.

When asked about the effect of the practice, Bev said she felt good; that she felt lighter, more relaxed and effortless. She described it as a feeling of 'floating', a real sense of calm. She had also become more observant, noticing things more readily, giving an example of how she had noticed the vivid colours on a red dress. This was quite different to her usual experience in which these sorts of thing went unnoticed.

Bev described how she found it difficult to stop her unintentional thinking from distracting her. It became apparent that she was practising the exercise for about five minutes, which is quite a challenge. We reminded ourselves that the practice only needs a minute or two and that the execution of bringing the mind to conscious presence is the key factor.

We then explored the phobia itself, discovering some significant insights in the process. When turning right across an intersection, going round a traffic island or having someone drive behind her, Bev would have a panic attack, with her mind racing with repetitive thoughts that 'I am in the way' or 'I am going to cause a crash'. At no point did Bev consciously choose to think these 'thoughts' – they arose habitually.

Another interesting insight related to a circumstantial change in her capacity to drive. Some years back, when Bev's BMW went in for a service and she was given a Mini-Cooper as a replacement, she found she was able to drive. It became apparent that, while her BMW was an automatic, the Mini had a manual transmission, which, being less familiar, required more concentration on her part when driving. The effect was fundamental and she was able to drive.

The manual transmission distracted Bev from her preoccupation with her conditioned thoughts about what other drivers thought about her driving and whether she was going to cause an accident. She simply did not have time to think about all that stuff. With the return of the Beamer, however, her doubt quickly resumed within the more familiar environment. We speculated that if she had kept the Mini, her monkey-mind would get up to its tricks once again as soon as she had mastered the manual gear change. The transitory improvement afforded by the Mini was short lived and reflected nothing more than circumstantial confidence.

When exploring what actually happened at the peak of a panic attack, Bev described how her heart rate would increase; she would breathe faster, fidget and hang on to the steering wheel to the extent that her knuckles would go white. In an attempt to drown out her thinking she would turn up the radio. Getting hot and bothered, Bev would open the window to cool down. What followed was an overwhelming desire to stop the car and run away – an avoidance strategy.

When asked about preliminary signals preceding a panic attack, Bev described how, when someone drove up behind her for example, she would be confronted with a barrage of thoughts in her mind. Unintentional, conditioned thoughts such as 'people push you to drive faster'; 'I am holding them up'; 'they are getting annoyed with me'; 'I am in their way' and the like, exacerbated her anxiety and undermined her capacity to drive. Bev's reality would become consumed by that way of thinking. The critical factor was the fact that Bev never consciously chose to think those thoughts; they just arose habitually.

When asked, 'Who is having these thoughts?', it became apparent that Bev assumed that it was herself, that 'these are my thoughts', 'I am having these thoughts'. Her underlying belief was 'I am these thoughts', an *ego-identity*. It was apparent that Bev was very consumed by and attached to this pseudo-thinking, identifying herself in the process.

When asked, 'who is observing the thoughts and feelings', Bev was able to recognise that something within was able to observe all that was going on. So one alternative was to stay on autopilot and become hooked into the mental and emotional hijacking. Another alternative was to detach herself from the conditioned pseudo-thinking and not take it too seriously, recognising it for the mindless and transitory distraction it was.

As her understanding and awareness increased, Bev described how she could either become 'trapped inside her mind' or see the hijacking from the perspective of the conscious observer – as if she was 'looking at myself from above'. The increased conscious awareness and detachment enabled a conscious choice as to her behaviour, her thoughts and feelings. With increased composure, her confidence to drive began to emerge quite naturally.

Other practices were also introduced. With the *statement of positive intent*, Bev replaced the irrational ideas such as 'I can't drive' and 'I'm going to cause an accident' with the more rational assertion that 'I can do this'.

## Session Three

In the third session, Bev described how she had managed to drive four or five times around the block, beginning each drive with the exercise of awareness. While difficult at first, the drive became easier with practice.

Regarding *practising conscious awareness*, Bev described how that initial feeling of floating or euphoria was no longer so apparent to her. This, we agreed, was inevitable as the experience became more familiar to her and that it was also very much related to the quality of her practice. While the floating had abated, Bev was sensing a growing calm in her life in general in that 'everything was beginning to slow down'. She was becoming more aware of how anxious she was in different situations and the effect of this.

During this part of the conversation, Bev went on to say: 'I feel stronger' and 'I have control of my anxiety'. This was a critical moment. At the heart of a panic attack is the fear of losing control. It is not the situation that causes the distress. It is the fear of not being in control of ourselves that is so immensely incapacitating. Bev was beginning to discover that *practising conscious awareness* was enabling her to stop 'thinking too much', and preventing her 'from overreacting emotionally' – the two essential factors related to self-control. Bev felt she was able to understand what was happening to her. She was beginning to believe that the phobia was something she could overcome.

Bev described an example when someone drove up behind her and she noticed a panic attack coming on. Rather than subject herself to the trickery of the monkey-mind, the assertion that 'they can just wait' came to her mind – a statement of positive intent. In this way, Bev took her attention away from the negative pseudo-thinking and focused it on the activity of driving itself.

In these many ways we were building a positive experience associated with driving and displacing negativity in the process.

Part of this involved having a light touch with all this serious stuff. The intention was not to belittle it in any way; it was to avoid a serious, self-critical stance. The practice was to laugh things off, successes and failures, without taking them too seriously. To laugh things off is to be detached, independent. Confidence has nothing to do with results and everything to do with our state and ability to *deal with things as they arise*.

*By this stage Bev had a range of practices at her disposal, which included: practising conscious awareness, pause to connect, connected attention, self-observation, statement of positive intent, a light touch and visualisation.*

At the end of the session, I asked Bev how she saw herself taking what she had already achieved to the next level. What arose out of this conversation was her firm resolve that 'I can do this' – but to take steps at her own pace as and when she was ready. This measured steadiness turned out to be critical, as it freed Bev from any self-imposed pressure to deliver results for which she was not yet ready. By letting go of the outcome, she was able to focus her attention on the practices at the *moment-of-impact*. The results would follow naturally – and so they did.

### Session Four

As a problem with Bev's car had kept her from driving that week, the fourth session turned out to be a short catch-up session. During our conversation it became apparent that Bev had kept the practices going in other aspects of her life and that her inner calm continued to grow. Bev described herself, saying, 'I'm usually very emotional,' but that this was 'not so intense now'; that she felt 'more in control', taking things 'more rationally' and 'not so badly'. She described a general sense of 'feeling more myself'.

Bev's final comment during this short session related to the practice of *connected attention*. She commented that this was 'easier said than done', that 'we do not have as much conscious control over our faculties as we might think'. She did, however, confirm that she was continuing to notice things a lot more, which was an excellent indication that her level of conscious awareness was increasing or, more accurately, allowing her greater access to the conscious presence that was already available to her in full measure.

**Session Five**

Amongst other things, session five focused on a not-so-pleasant experience Bev had when attempting to make a right turn across an intersection. It did not go well and Bev described how she 'felt disappointed' in herself. Central to this, however, was the insight that 'the more I think about it' the more the fear and doubt prevailed. The critical success here was that Bev was beginning to notice with increased ease the inner workings of her mind and heart, and the effect that these were having, without any dependency on anyone else. She was in the driving seat, independent, with all that she needed to bring about the changes that she felt were necessary. No one else could do that for her. The support from me, her coach, was in helping her to discover what was already there.

On a more positive note, Bev described a situation when she had needed to book a flight to Florida for her forthcoming holiday. To do this, she needed to borrow her sister's car and drive home and then back to work again. This experience demonstrated that the principles and practices were working and she was able to make the journey without a hitch. She also recognised that the urgent need to book the flight and driving a different car acted as distractions from all her usual doubts and fears about driving.

Another interesting revelation was the fact that her husband, John, was very supportive, driving her around whenever needed. While clearly not his intention, John's support was actually part of the problem as it provided Bev with a substantial avoidance strategy. The session closed with an agreed plan of action with regards to this avoidance strategy, as well as with her forthcoming holiday to Florida.

**Session Six**

Having arrived back from her holiday, Bev reported that she had managed to spend some time driving in Florida. This provided another positive association with driving, the sweet taste of success. We reflected on the fact that in the US people drive on the right hand side of the road and that this unfamiliar change meant that Bev's monkey-mind had less time to 'think' and interfere – as was the case with the manual transmission in the Mini-Cooper.

*Conscious breathing* was introduced as a practice to help Bev deal with oncoming panic attacks. As an attack would be difficult to stop once it had gathered momentum, the trick was for her to start the practice as soon as the initial signals became apparent. The critical factor was to come off autopilot and into the conscious present so as to observe the early signals as soon as possible.

Bev commented, 'I bring it on myself.' That was a critical insight. In no way was Bev a victim, with panic attacks being imposed on her in some way. The fact was that the panic attacks were created and recreated by none other than herself. With the double-edged sword of knowledge and awareness, Bev had everything she needed to deal with them when it really mattered.

Bev was beginning to realise that 'I can do anything with the car'. As soon as the early signals began to emerge, the practices provided the means to deal with the attack. By giving her conscious attention to the conscious present, she made it impossible for the pseudo-thinking to exist and undermine her performance potential. In the absence of self-imposed doubt, her confidence released naturally from within.

With regards to the avoidance strategy involving Bev's husband, we discussed how, given the strength of their relationship, John could talk Bev through difficult moments in his naturally calm and reassuring manner. By giving her attention to the sound of John's voice, Bev would free herself from the tyranny of the monkey-mind by focusing on something in the here-and-now.

Central to our conversation were Bev's comments concerning the impact the practices had had on her life in general. These she described as having a 'wonderful effect on my life', that it was 'the most positive and amazing thing I have ever learnt', which motivated her to practise whenever possible. In fact, Bev mentioned that, while on holiday in the US, she did not get caught up in family dramas as she typically would. People actually commented on how much more calm and composed she had become.

At the end of the session, Bev's statement of positive intent was 'stuff it, I can do this' and 'I feel like this could happen'. In this way, the mystery of her driving phobia was beginning to lift.

## Session Seven

The seventh session began with Bev describing how she had managed to drive each day since the previous session, with several right turns across intersections. She described how she had dealt with a panic attack the previous day through *conscious breathing* and *connected attention*. Bev commented, 'I can live with that tiny bit of panic.' The tangible improvements clearly had their effect and Bev was really beginning to enjoy her driving again.

On another occasion, Bev said she just could not take a right turn and, rather than self-recrimination, her response within was simply, 'that's OK.' She dealt with it with a light touch, focusing on the more positive side of the experience.

Bev again commented on the general impact that her new knowledge and awareness were having on her life, saying, 'I am generally happier in my life,' and, 'I am not as anxious about everything,' but very much 'more relaxed in myself' and 'so much calmer about everything in my life'. In essence, what Bev had achieved was that: 'I've stopped giving myself such a hard time generally.'

Bev did acknowledge that she had not always taken opportunities to drive, allowing John to drive instead. She feared being humiliated in front of her husband. Well, by now this was a familiar pattern and, given what had been achieved, this was a piece of cake for her to deal with. When asked what was behind her fear, Bev commented, 'I feel anxious about what he will think.' So the monkey-mind was raising its head once again – but happily the principles and practices provided all she needed to deal with this form of self-doubt.

## Session Eight

At the start of the eighth session, Bev was delighted to report that she had taken her husband out in the car several times and, although it had felt scary the first time, it became much easier.

Driving both her own car and her husband's 4x4, she described how the practices enabled her to manage her state, sustaining a calm composure and doing 'loads of right turns' in the process. She described how driving with John helped him become more aware of what she was going through. This helped to alleviate her self-criticism. The fact that she found driving with John to be fun and relaxing made quite a difference.

Bev continued commenting that 'every time I drive I feel progress'. She was also feeling that she 'wanted to drive a bit more'. When out shopping with John one day, Bev spontaneously found herself saying, 'I'll drive.' Yes! What a result!

While we reflected on the transformational process Bev had been going through, it became apparent that something was missing from the conversation. When asked, Bev was completely at a loss as to what that was. Throughout our entire conversation, at no time had Bev mentioned anything about anxiety, nerves or panic attacks. Her response was priceless when she casually said, 'Oh, the signs have come up and I distracted myself and breathed through these,' adding, 'If people have to wait they'll just have to wait.' The general sense was that her panic attacks were no longer relevant, that she had the confidence to deal with them when it really mattered.

Looking to stretch the development even further, I asked Bev to rate what she'd achieved on a scale of one to ten. She said that when we started she was at one and now she felt she was at five, which I thought was quite harsh – if not for her, for me, but that is an ego thing and not relevant. Looking to stretch her performance further still, I asked Bev what she'd like to achieve and her response was that, 'I want to get into my car and not give it a second thought,' and so we explored what would get her to a seven.

**Session Nine**

In our final session we consolidated what had been covered and achieved throughout the coaching process. We also identified what would help Bev to sustain and build on her achievements. Approximately nine weeks earlier, Bev had begun the coaching process with a full-blown driving phobia and a real crisis in confidence. Through the tenacious application of the principles and practices, she had moved to the point at which she was driving regularly and, more importantly, had discovered within herself an inner sense of certainty that she could observe and deal with her fear and doubt in the Stretch Zone when it really mattered. Bev was feeling confident and happy both as a driver and in her day-to-day life.

Some months after the coaching, I got in touch with Bev to see how things were going. I also asked her for a reference and this is what she said:

> 'I would have no hesitation in recommending Glenn as a coach. He is highly professional, with a wonderful mixture of a cool, relaxed approach and a deep understanding of human behaviour. I had been struggling with a driving phobia for many years and had tried various methods of help, none of which had worked. Glenn's approach enabled me to see where the 'fear' really lay, helping me to see the issue in a different and less serious way. My 'fear' of driving and in life in general has subsided. Some months have passed since the coaching and I am still on the road, driving!'
>
> Bev

# Conclusion

We so often make the mistake of believing statements such as 'I am not a confident person' or that confidence is 'something I lack and need to learn and acquire', thereby unintentionally incarcerating ourselves in false beliefs. Trapped within the self-imposed prison of our waking dream, we become the convicts of our own convictions and seldom pause to question our self-deception and outcast state.

In our hijacked desperation, our knee-jerk reaction all too often takes the form of a whole lot of frenetic *doing*, in the deluded hope that we can somehow fill our apparent emptiness with the sort of misguided confidence-boosting hype that goes with the idea of *having confidence*. Distrusting ourselves, we try to be everything we are not, psyching ourselves up in our conditioned ways and hoping against hope that we can disguise and suppress our fears and doubts through adopting a mask of pseudo-confidence.

However, the effort that goes into sporting a mask of pseudo-confidence actually drains our energy and depletes our capacity for action, allowing mistaken convictions such as 'I am not a confident person' to limit even further our paradigm about who and what really we are. Within the murky outlook that is characteristic of an exiled state of autopilot, we have no perspective from which to observe our confusion and we continue to drink from this poisoned chalice as fewer and fewer options appear open to us.

Yet, we have seen, there is a completely different option – an alternative paradigm that is charged with uncharted potentiality and unknown possibilities. Confidence is not an object that we can *have* or an action that we can *do*. Confidence is a state, an inherent and imminent potential for every human being without exception. As a state, it is not a question of *having confidence*, but of *being confident*.

*Being confident* is about being ourselves and about being true to ourselves above all else. When we remember ourselves, with all our unfathomed potentiality, and accept ourselves simply as we are, then we will truly begin to trust and enjoy ourselves, even when we find ourselves facing the Stretch Zone in anxious trepidation. Whenever we exit our waking dream through our conscious presence in the present moment, thereby creating the conditions within which genuine confidence becomes inevitable, a reservoir of confidence, our birthright, will be released from within ourselves in limitless abundance, anywhere, anytime.

To sum up in only a few words, confidence is our natural state. Confidence is the absence of doubt. Confidence is a state of detached interest. Confidence is a heightened state of readiness to unleash the undetermined potentiality that lies brimming at the threshold of our Stretch Zone. The fearless courage and confidence that arise within us when we step out of our comfort zone into the Stretch Zone bring with them everything we need to face our most feared and treasured apprehensions.

Trust yourself! Never doubt yourself! You have everything you need to face any adversity that comes your way in your life's journey. All you need to do is to trust yourself and step up into the Stretch Zone. When you no longer hold yourself back, your potentiality and Nature will take care of the rest.

At every crossroads we face in our lives, we can choose the small and petty path of the *inner idiot*, who, in spite of its relentless sound and fury, signifies little more than nothing as it struts and frets its hour upon life's stage in its ignorant impotence. Alternatively, we can make a conscious choice to pause within our innermost being and enter into the realm of the *inner sage*, full of wisdom, temperance and resolute intention. You only have to trust yourself!

Like the rest of us, you have absolutely no idea of the depth of your being and capability. You will only fathom your depths if you dive deep into uncharted waters, shedding your self-imposed ideas about who and what you are along the way.

*Being confident* is not really the issue. The real challenge is what you will do with your confidence once you have begun to master it. Confidence can so easily be used with the selfish intent that is characteristic of the *inner idiot*: to better our lot at the expense of others. A more rewarding option is to offer your confidence in service of the greater good of all, the only lasting goodness for humanity as a species.

Make no mistake; you are already confident in full measure! The Stretch Zone awaits you. As you approach it, what choice will you make today?

# Exciting Opportunities @ www.widelko.com

As a writer, coach and learning facilitator Glenn loves what he does – creating opportunities for people to step across the threshold of their potentiality – discovering their best in The Stretch Zone.

Opportunities, current and forthcoming, to support you in exploring the ideas in The Stretch Zone further and applying them in your life are available on: www.widelko.com/stretchzone.

- Stretch Zone – E-Course
- Stretch Zone – Research Questionnaire
- Stretch Zone – Self-Assessment
- Stretch Zone – Inspirational MP3s
- Stretch Zone – Case Studies
- Stretch Zone – 360
- Stretch Zone – Coaching
- Stretch Zone – Workshop
- Stretch Zone – Signature Talk

To find out more about Glenn's inspirational training programmes specialising in the following areas, visit www.widelko.com/training.

- Leadership & Management Development
- Self-Awareness & Self-Mastery
- Relationship Management
- Communication, Conflict & Influencing
- Coaching & Performance Management
- Teamwork

You are welcome to get in touch to find out more about our coaching or training or how you can bring The Stretch Zone to life in your organisation or in your life personally and professionally.

- Email: glenn@widelko.com
- Website: www.widelko.com
- Blog: www.widelko.com/blog
- Linked In: www.linkedin.com/in/glennwidelko

'As a facilitator Glenn leads you to push yourself to places you didn't know existed within you. I have never known any other personal development experience that leaves you feeling so challenged – a hugely beneficial investment, both personally and professionally.'

**John McParland, Director of Business Banking**